Devotions for Christian Educators

That they may have LIFE

David J. Bangert

Northwestern Publishing House
Milwaukee, Wisconsin

Cover photos: Corbis, Design Pics
Art Director: Karen Knutson
Cover Design: Carianne Ciriacks

Scripture is taken from the HOLY BIBLE, NEW INTERNATIONAL VERSION®. NIV®. Copyright © 1973, 1978, 1984 by International Bible Society. Used by permission of Zondervan. All rights reserved.

The "NIV" and "New International Version" trademarks are registered in the United States Patent and Trademark Office by International Bible Society. Use of either trademark requires the permission of International Bible Society.

All rights reserved. This publication may not be copied, photocopied, reproduced, translated, or converted to any electronic or machine-readable form in whole or in part, except for brief quotations, without prior written approval from the publisher.

Library of Congress Control Number: 2007929765
Northwestern Publishing House
1250 N. 113th St., Milwaukee, WI 53226-3284
www.nph.net
© 2008 by Northwestern Publishing House
Published 2008
Printed in the United States of America
ISBN 978-0-8100-2057-3

To Jean, who has shown me what it is to be a caring, loving, Christian teacher.

Contents

Preface ix
When Little Things Become Big 1
Are You Ready for the Whitewater? 4
Your Will Be Done 7
Free to Serve 10
Do You Deserve a Break Today? 12
That They May Have Life 15
All One Body, We 17
It's Not About Me 20
He Is Our God; We Are His People 23
Growing in the Lord 25
Homecoming 28
In Love, Helping One Another 30
Your Will, Not Mine, O Lord 32
Celebrating the Reformation 34
A Caring, Christian Community 36
Alive in God's Promise 38
It's Only a Game 40
Hope Alive 43
Blinded by My Vision 45
A Cloudy Thanksgiving 48
Saying "Thank You" Too Much 51
In the Light of His Love 53

A Mighty Fortress Lying in a Manger	56
I Can Wait for Christmas	58
God's Secret: Christ Is in You	61
Open Our Eyes, Lord	64
Don't Touch That Contrast Button!	67
Lift High the Cross	70
Don't Sleep In!	72
A New Year's Resolution	74
Walk in Wisdom	77
The Upside of Anger	79
Set Free by the Truth	82
Teach Us Your Ways, O Lord	85
Saint Titus and the January Doldrums	87
Press On Toward the Goal	89
Am I the Weeds?	92
Soaring in the Spirit	94
Reenrollment Night—Not for Everyone	96
Shine Like Stars	98
'Tis Good, Lord, to Be Here	101
Looking Forward	104
Building Our Faith and Our Future	106
Know Christ, or Know What Christ Wants?	109
Set Your Mind on Things Above	112
March Madness	114
The Lord Is My Shepherd	117

Dad, Teacher, Saint? 119

Be Strong and Courageous 121

What's Your Name? 124

Why Are You Here? 126

The Majesty of Holy Week 128

More Than Conquerors 130

Ups and Downs 132

Looking Ahead 134

Rejoice in the Lord 136

Cheer Up! 139

We Proclaim Christ 141

Serve as Jesus Served 144

An Audience of One 147

Upheld by His Hand 150

They Just Don't Get It! 153

Is Enough Ever Enough? 156

Running Out of Time 158

Celebrate God's Grace 160

Forward in Faith 162

A Different Kind of Commencement 164

For Such a Time as This 167

Where's My Reward? 169

Say What? 172

Embrace Them; Then Let Them Go 175

Preface

Why write devotions? Better yet, why read devotions? Doesn't it seem that a professional church worker's life is already full of God? With Christian coworkers, chapel services, a curriculum permeated with a biblical perspective, and the constant reminders of God in our workday and workplace, a devotional life might not seem that necessary. Yet it is that very sense of complacency that should spur us on to a more devotional life.

Satan doesn't need to spend a lot of time with those who don't know Christ; he already has them in his back pocket. It is those of us on the frontline—those charged with bringing the good news of Jesus to God's young people—that Satan targets. The tactics he uses are subtle: job dissatisfaction, tensions with coworkers, disappointment over a failed lesson, a student gone bad, bickering over funding, scheduling, professional turf, the inordinate amount of time spent away from family, or just the false sense of invulnerability that comes from being a church worker.

And that's where a devotional life fits in. Devotional reading can strengthen and enrich our spiritual conversations with others. It can give us a deeper reverence for God's inspired Word. It establishes a disciplined routine for studying God's Word and speaking to him often in prayer. It links faith to the cycles of the church year and the school year. In short, the devotional life makes faith flourish. Surely we want that for our own lives. And we also want that for the lives of the young people we serve.

I started writing these devotions more than three years ago because I saw a need for all of those things in my own life. Throughout the process I did feel God speaking to me as I struggled, or rejoiced, at particular moments in my own ministry. At first I tried to write to high school teachers because I hadn't seen much written for them. As time went on, I realized that the challenges of being a teacher in a Lutheran school are similar regardless of the students' ages. I also realized that most of these challenges are experienced by all Christians, not just those of us in education.

I want to thank my wife, Jean, who has always supported me beyond duty's call. The fact that God placed her in my life is no accident. I see him working through her each and every day. I also want to thank my fellow faculty members for being the live guinea pigs for these devotions. Their feedback has been invaluable.

The phrase used in the title of this book, *That They May Have Life,* comes from John 10:10. There Jesus says, "I have come that they may have life, and have it to the full." The *they* that he is speaking about are all people who belong to him in faith. Through his Word and sacraments, we are given a glimpse of that full life now and the sure promise of its final fullness in eternity. You and I are committed to sharing that good news with those of the next generation. May the readings that follow encourage you for this awesome and wonderful privilege during the coming school year so that through you and your work, they too may have life.

When Little Things Become Big

. . . Then Nathan said to David, "You are the man! . . . Why did you despise the word of the Lord by doing what is evil in his eyes? You struck down Uriah the Hittite with the sword and took his wife to be your own. You killed him with the sword of the Ammonites. . . ."

Then David said to Nathan, "I have sinned against the Lord."

Nathan replied, "The Lord has taken away your sin. You are not going to die. But because by doing this you have made the enemies of the Lord show utter contempt, the son born to you will die." *2 Samuel 12:1-14*

    A couple of weeks ago I backed my car into our basketball hoop's pole. Needless to say, the pole won. I managed to collect myself (after declaring myself to be one of the most stupid drivers who ever lived) and drove away before inspecting the damage.

    That night, mustering all the male bravado I could, I said to Jean, "Well, it's not too bad, I don't think it should cost that much." Two estimates later I realized how wrong I was. Both estimates were much higher than I had anticipated. To make matters worse, I couldn't shake the fact that it was the same pole I'd been reminding everyone else in the family to be careful about. So there were subtle implications I hadn't even thought of when the incident happened.

    Many of my sins are like that. A careless word or action hurts people more than I could imagine. Trying to get away with something often leads to consequences never considered. Acting before thinking quite often leaves me with regrets. The repetition of what I might have once considered small sins can lead to larger sins and habitual sinning that brings my whole faith relationship with God into question.

In dealing with people and students, I can think of times I've said something that left people with a wrong impression—an impression that led to deeper misunderstandings and confusion. A little throwaway statement can cause big problems.

King David ran into the same problems in his life. When he gave in to temptation and slept with Bathsheba, David failed to consider all the problems his behavior would create for so many people. And the more he tried to undo the problems he had created, the more problems he caused.

In his great love for David, God knew just how to handle both the sins and the problems that resulted from those sins. He sent his prophet Nathan to communicate with David.

Notice Nathan's words in verse 13; David really needed to hear this: "The LORD has taken away your sin." Then, without skipping a beat, Nathan let David know that there would still be consequences for what he had done. David had no one to blame but himself. Worse, the things he had done were things he would have told others not to do.

I'm not trying to equate running into a pole with what David did. But the results of my action and the resulting consequences of my many sins have caused many problems of their own. That is why the words of Nathan have an impact on me.

When God says, "I forgive you," it changes everything. I can move on with my life, free of the nagging guilt connected to my foolish sins. Even the consequences serve a different purpose than to punish me; they remind me that, for Jesus' sake, things are right in my relationship with God. Each day they help me remember my own human shortcomings and flaws, and then I am again reminded of God's abundant grace.

As you have time to reflect during these remaining days of summer, may you also know the joy of Christ's forgiveness. And through the strength that his forgiveness gives you, may you understand the consequences of sin in your life in a way that brings testimony to your faith relationship with him who loves us.

Preparing for a New School Year

Are You Ready for the Whitewater?

Finally, be strong in the Lord and in his mighty power. Put on the full armor of God so that you can take your stand against the devil's schemes. For our struggle is not against flesh and blood, but against the rulers, against the authorities, against the powers of this dark world and against the spiritual forces of evil in the heavenly realms. Therefore put on the full armor of God, so that when the day of evil comes, you may be able to stand your ground, and after you have done everything, to stand. Stand firm then, with the belt of truth buckled around your waist, with the breastplate of righteousness in place, and with your feet fitted with the readiness that comes from the gospel of peace. In addition to all this, take up the shield of faith, with which you can extinguish all the flaming arrows of the evil one. Take the helmet of salvation and the sword of the Spirit, which is the word of God. And pray in the Spirit on all occasions with all kinds of prayers and requests. With this in mind, be alert and always keep on praying for all the saints.
Ephesians 6:10-18

This past June I had the opportunity to go whitewater rafting with my sons and one of my cousins. We were the only passengers on a three-hour trip down Cripple Creek outside Denver. Of course, we had a guide. I don't think we could have safely made it without him.

You may be looking at the new school year as if it were a whitewater rafting adventure of your own. Maybe circumstances in your life make it seem like a wild ride is ahead. Consider the similarities. As we prepared for our trip, we were each outfitted with a wet suit, a helmet, a lifejacket, and an oar. If you and I are not properly outfitted for this school year, or for life, we will not be ready for the challenges that we will have to face. Have you invited God and his Spirit to fit you with the necessary equipment for the challenges ahead? Take the time to read Ephesians chapter 6 before you start the school year.

Our next step was to have a 20-minute lecture on what to do if we fell out of the boat. In many ways this was a sermon on how to handle unexpected challenges. If we fell out, we were supposed to relax, float through the water, and wait for the others to rescue us. If we tried to rescue ourselves, we were assured we would get into even bigger trouble. Sound familiar? There's always the temptation to do everything ourselves and not accept help from others. Christ works through our faculties, our families, and our friends. How about letting them help in the struggles and unexpected challenges you will encounter ahead?

Working as a five-man team, we needed to learn to listen to, trust, and obey our guide. He knew how to help us through the rough spots. God is a lot like that guide. Through his Word he gives us directions on how to handle the rapids. Through his love and forgiveness he encourages us when all appears to be lost. Through his discipline he teaches us to listen and obey. Yet God doesn't live our lives for us. He expects us to forge ahead. He's been through the rapids, sending his Son to experience the same pain and suffering we are experiencing in life. He is the guide; we need to place our confidence in him in calm waters and in rough. He knows where dangerous places are and how to handle them. Listen to him and trust in his direction when whitewater is approaching.

Then we were off. There were five major rapids we had to traverse. It was fun and challenging. I look back now and wonder how we ever made it through. Life and a school year can be like that. What we fear will be insurmountable ends up being no more than a blip. Other times, in retrospect, we can't believe how serious a situation was once we have finally moved on. In both cases it is God who makes the difference. When we truly trust in him and his plans for us, we really can handle any situation.

In the end, we all survived the adventure. I have the spectacular photos to prove it. But we also all knew that without our guide we would have been in trouble. That was the first and most important lesson of our whitewater experience. Fit yourself with the right equipment; let others help you when you need it; listen to the word of the guide.

Have a great year—the ride of a lifetime. Look forward to it, trusting in the ultimate whitewater-rafting guide.

Beginning a New School Year

Your Will Be Done

"Your Father knows what you need before you ask him. This, then, is how you should pray: 'Our Father in heaven, hallowed be your name, your kingdom come, your will be done on earth as it is in heaven. Give us today our daily bread. Forgive us our debts, as we also have forgiven our debtors. And lead us not into temptation, but deliver us from the evil one.'" *Matthew 6:8-13*

My sister was going to fly up from Florida to visit us over the Labor Day weekend. Crammed into the tight weekend schedule were plans to watch my son play in a college football game. A little thing called Hurricane Frances got in the way. My sister's plane was grounded. Everyone involved was really disappointed.

The enrollment at our school dipped a little this year, and we had to make some really tough staffing decisions. Those involved were really stressed and disappointed.

Each year I have taught, there has been at least one student in our school who has lost a parent in death. Everyone involved is always very saddened.

Each year that I've been in education, I've tried to figure out where my life is going. Annually, I am disappointed and distressed when I don't get the answers I want.

There are people you and I know who struggle daily with sickness, hardship, or decision-making that saddens and disappoints them and the people who love them.

"Your will be done"? It's a phrase used by some when faced with situations like the ones I've just mentioned. I have to confess that I don't always buy into that often-repeated mantra of the Christian. I know the good, Christian thing to do is to accept life and its challenges and disappointments with the idea that God has some greater plan for us that uses all of these challenges for our good. Maybe it's lack of faith on my part, but I don't think that's part of God's will for me.

I think we walk on dangerous ground when we fatalistically write off every bad thing in our lives as part of God's will. I believe God's will for me is always good. He loves me and wants only good things for me. Theology 101 tells us that the bad things in life are caused by sin and its consequences. My little brain has trouble with the logic that says that the person who loves me as much as he loves his own Son would utilize sin so that his will can be done in my life.

An old hymn written by Samuel Rodigast begins with the words "What God ordains is always good." Isn't that what we're praying for here, that God's will would overcome the will of Satan and his dominion? Instead of using the words "Your will be done" as an excuse to push away our own shortcomings, we should consider actively working for God's will to be done. That may mean a closer examination of our own lives and the role sin plays in them. It certainly means expressing the gospel message through our dealings with students, coworkers, parents, and neighbors.

We will have challenges, disappointments, and tragedies this school year. Any educator who doesn't understand that is in for a rough year. What we all need to know is that we can work toward filling the painful void those occurrences create. We can do the work of filling those voids with God's love, by remembering God's call to us in our baptisms, and by praying for constant renewal of his Spirit in our lives.

When we do those things, we are putting the words "Your will be done" into action rather than using them as a convenient, it's-out-of-my-hands excuse when things don't go our way.

The next time you hear, or pray, the words "Your will be done," consider the significance they have for your life. God has called you to be one of his ambassadors on earth. What a privilege! What an opportunity! Pray for the courage and power to work for his will to be done.

> What God ordains is always good;
> This truth remains unshaken.
> Though sorrow, need, or death be mine,
> I shall not be forsaken.
> I fear no harm,
> For with his arm
> He will embrace and shield me;
> So to my God I yield me.
>
> *Samuel Rodigast*

Early School Year

Free to Serve

"I know your deeds, your love and faith, your service and perseverance, and that you are now doing more than you did at first." *Revelation 2:19*
"Whoever loses his life for my sake will find it."
Matthew 10:39

Freedom is a word that is easily thrown about these days. It's a word that conjures up different ideas in different people. And we would probably all agree that it's a concept that deserves to be valued, no matter how we define it. However, the idea of freedom and service in the same sentence doesn't seem to make logical sense at first glance.

In the late '60s a singer by the name of Janis Joplin sang a song that included the lyrics "Freedom's just another word for nothing left to lose." For some inexplicable reason, those words have always resonated in my mind. I really don't know if Joplin was a Christian—she didn't exactly espouse a Christian lifestyle as she was well-known for her taste for Southern Comfort during concerts and died from a drug overdose. However, her words from this song make me think about Christian freedom. In essence, when I see that I have nothing left to lose, then I experience the freedom that is mine in Christ.

When I understand that the things this world values are not important and that my relationship with Christ is the most important thing in my life, then I begin to be truly free from the burdens of this life. Conversely, when I become absorbed with this life's burdens, I become absorbed with myself and am less likely to serve my Lord.

The beginning of a school year seems to bring with it too many things to do—lots of late nights and no time to finish our preparations. What should be a time of excitement can easily degenerate into weariness. I really don't feel free; I feel worn down by a yoke of *have-to-dos* rather than enjoying *want-to-dos.* That's when I need to remember that the power and joy in my life comes from him who sets me free from the greatest burden, which is sin.

When I remember to daily embrace the freedom that is mine through Baptism and the power of the Spirit, then the experience of freedom returns to my life. And that freedom really does mean I've got nothing left to lose; everything is then eclipsed by the joy of knowing Christ.

Maybe that's what was happening to the church members at Thyatira whom John was addressing in the passage from Revelation. As they received the power of the Spirit and began to understand the meaning of freedom in Christ, their lives reflected it more each passing day. Our students need to see that in us—the joy and excitement for life that comes from the freedom we have in Christ.

And isn't that what we long to see in our students? That same sort of joy in life that only Christ offers—a joy that frees us all to serve one another?

As we journey through this school year together, let us pray that all of us turn our freedom into service for him who gave us the freedom. And perhaps as this year comes to a close, we may all be blessed to hear someone say, "You are now doing more than you did at first."

General

Do You Deserve a Break Today?

I am the least of the apostles and do not even deserve to be called an apostle, because I persecuted the church of God. But by the grace of God I am what I am, and his grace to me was not without effect. No, I worked harder than all of them—yet not I, but the grace of God that was with me. Whether, then, it was I or they, this is what we preach, and this is what you believed. *1 Corinthians 15:9-11*

This past summer my wife and I took a cruise to celebrate our 25th anniversary. If you've ever been on a cruise or to an all-inclusive resort, you know that you're surrounded by a seemingly endless array of food, drink, entertainment, and leisure choices. At meals you can have one of everything if you'd like. It's not unusual to have the prime rib and the lobster tail. We were surrounded by the message that we should overdo it, because, after all, we deserved it.

Then last week the two of us were visiting McDonalds for breakfast before school (a little once-a-week tradition we started years ago when we still had kids at home). On the wall was a poster suggesting that I indulge myself with one of their many fantastic dessert creations. (What is a McFlurry anyhow?) Well, I managed to limit myself to an Egg McMuffin, but the message was clear—after everything, I still deserved at least an apple pie from McDonalds.

It got me thinking about what I really do deserve. I think all of us, in rare moments of humility, will say we don't deserve everything we have. I have two great sons, a loving wife, supportive relatives, a nice house, cars, coworkers who genuinely care, a job, and all kinds of stuff that I would be hard-pressed to justify. Yet if I'm really honest, there is a part of me that does think I deserve it all. I'm the one who has spent his whole life in Lutheran schools. I'm the one who's tried not to complain about how little I'm paid or what's expected from a teacher. I'm the one who tries to go to church every week, put my envelope in the collection plate, and not complain too much about worship styles. So when I balance them out, I often have trouble escaping my deep, dark secret: I do believe I deserve more. Maybe next time I will order a triple-thick milkshake and have two lobster tails!

The trouble with this is that I'm really not the person who does all of the good I perceive myself doing. It is "by the grace of God I am what I am." Paul's words echo through my life as a constant reminder of what my life really is—nothing without Christ. Each time I come face-to-face with my own inadequacies and sins, I am given the chance, by God's grace, to step back from the brink of despair to be filled with the joy of his love for me. What I truly deserve is the utter hopelessness that comes from knowing just how wretched a sinner I am. What I deserve is God's just wrath and his eternal judgment. What I get instead is the word of forgiveness through God's abundant grace and mercy. And it isn't just one word. God's grace is a fountain that never stops flowing. His forgiveness is always there for me each time I sin.

Our pastor recently noted that following Hurricane Katrina, he heard people asking the question, Why do bad things happen to good people? His response to the question was that at its core, the question was based on an incorrect premise. By his reckoning there is no such thing as good people. Then he explained that by nature we are all marred by our sin and thus are immoral creatures. But as believers in Christ, we never get what we deserve and we never deserve what we get. None of this comes about by our own doing. All of this is ours only by God's grace.

Do I deserve all the blessings of my life? No. Nor do I deserve the spiritual gifts that God continues to pour into my life. They are only mine by God's grace. The same is true for you and for your students. So go ahead, treat yourself to that hot fudge sundae—just don't think you deserve it!

That They May Have Life

"The thief comes only to steal and kill and destroy; I have come that they may have life, and have it to the full."
John 10:10

    A few years ago I taught a class that dealt with dating, love, and marriage. The course came at the topics from the Christian perspective. One of the popular questions, not surprisingly, was "How do I know when I'm in love?" The standard answer I would give went something like this: "You're probably in love when you realize that the other person's happiness is more important than your own." For young people there's often a dreamy, romantic way of thinking about the other person that doesn't help much when it comes to clearheaded decision making. I wanted my students to think more about pushing personal desires to the background in their interpersonal relationships. Of course, there are a lot of other facets to being in love, but I thought that was one way for young people to think about it.

    Those of you who are parents understand how this same principle works. We frequently subjugate our own interests to the needs and interests of our children. We want them to be happy, and we're willing to sacrifice some of our own time, energy, money, etc., for them.

    Christ compares his actions with those of a thief to make a similar point. The thief's only thought is for his own desires. Christ, on the other hand, is more like a shepherd who loves and cares for his sheep. His only concern is for the safety and well-being of the members of his flock. He wants nothing more than that "they may have life." And he has made the ultimate sacrifice to achieve that goal.

As educators, we have chosen a profession that strives to create better lives for those whom we serve. It was part of the deal when we signed up. We understood that we would be asked to give up some personal time or that we would be asked to forfeit, or at least defer, some of our personal goals in order to give our students fuller lives. Sometimes we feel that we have to give up too much—or that too much is asked of us. It also becomes really hard when we don't see the results for which we had hoped. Then it is easy to wonder, *"Why should I give up so much for those students who don't seem to want to get it?"*

Jesus might have felt the same way about the people for whom he was dying. Thank God, he didn't. He persevered in reaching for his goal, which was to make sure we would have lives full to the brim with purpose and meaning, lives filled to overflowing with joy and peace in our relationships with him, now and forever.

As a Christian educator, I need to be reminded often of this big picture. A life without Christ is an empty life. A life with Christ is made full by his love. To be true to our calling, we must understand that through the power of God's Holy Spirit, we are here to help give our students lives to the fullest, which are lives filled with Jesus.

Find a way to share Jesus with your students. Even when it means you will have to make sacrifices, be the vessel of the Holy Spirit that shares his love . . . "that they may have life"!

All One Body, We

Over all these virtues put on love, which binds them all together in perfect unity. Colossians 3:14

It happens all the time. It starts in preschool; gathers momentum through elementary, middle, and high school; and really takes off when we're adults. You know what it's like. You're at a party or a conference or a meeting, and you subconsciously (or consciously) start rating yourself. You compare yourself to the other people in the room. Who rates higher than me? lower? I'm sure I'm more important than that person over there. The criteria are usually of our own making: intelligence, personality, appearance, communication skills. The list always fits the personal profile we have constructed in our own heads. Inevitably, we angle and maneuver this private little internal conversation until we come out on top.

Having been an educator in a high-school setting for many years has given me a close-up view of high-school kids fighting and clawing for status. But we're kidding ourselves if we don't think it happens with adults too. And it's not just in schools. It happens in the workplace too—and in families, congregations, even synods.

In the classroom it's easy to get carried away by all the power and authority that comes with being the teacher. Same thing with administrators. It's easy to forget that we are all part of one body. It's easy to let our own egocentric goals get the best of us. *"After all,"* I say to myself, *"I've worked hard to get to this posi-*

tion. I think I have earned my status. I really am more important than the person sitting next to me."

If I reflect that kind of thinking, how can I expect my students or coworkers to be any different?

The passage from Colossians was written by Paul at the end of a long list of qualities that he felt followers of Christ should have. The key to all of the qualities is love.

Love is the key to unity of any kind. The only time we forget about our own status is when we humble ourselves and put the interests of others before our own.

Notice the title of this devotion. I saw it once used as a theme for a school year. Instead of saying, "We are one body," it changes the words around. The statement then comes out as "All one body, we," which seems more forceful to me. It seems more inclusive, more demonstrative. That's what love does. Love binds people together. In other places in Scripture, love is described as peaceful and gentle, almost passive. But in this text, love carries a powerful force of its own. Love is an action. It binds people together as one body. A love so powerful that it can truly cause sinful, self-centered people to think and act and speak in unison is a very powerful kind of love. This kind of love can only be generated in the hearts of those who have experienced the power of God's loving forgiveness in their own lives.

If we are ever to be truly united in one body as Christ's own bride, we need to let God's love for us help us forget about status and concentrate on caring. Try that in your relationships this week. Put others first—your students, your family, your friends. Help bind your community together in Christ's love so that we can boldly say together, "All one body, we."

General

It's Not About Me

By him all things were created: things in heaven and on earth, visible and invisible, whether thrones or powers or rulers or authorities; all things were created by him and for him. He is before all things, and in him all things hold together. *Colossians 1:16,17*

The opening sentence of Rick Warren's best-seller *The Purpose Driven Life* states, "It's not about you." That must be a rude awakening for many of the people we come in contact with on any given day. Let me share some recent examples. This past summer I dealt with parents who pushed and pushed to get their kids in advanced classes, despite the fact that there was no evidence to support their claims that the kids should be in those classes. Parents, students, and teachers claim things to be unfair when they don't get what they want. Athletes don't bother to tell coaches that they'll miss practice and then let the whole team down as a result. Parents complain because their son or daughter wasn't mentioned in a news article in the school bulletin. I have been around coaches who seem to blame the team for everything that goes wrong and want all the credit when things go well. I have seen administrators who seem to revel in the amount of appointments and committees they can be on rather than in the mission as a whole. How about churches and schools who give the impression that the size of the congregation, or school, eclipses the mission?

And what about me? I seem to get easily caught up in a woe-is-me attitude because life isn't treating me fairly. (Whatever that means.) That attitude often causes me to lose sight of my calling and my reason for being. I find it so easy to expect the world to revolve around me. I find it so easy to assume my needs, my wants, and my expectations are more important. I find it so easy to believe I'm always right because I always know just a little bit more than anyone else. I find it so easy to let my life spiral into a completely myopic world in which everything is about me. It's a constant battle. Even when I know better, I really do believe it's all about me.

But why would I think that? Because that's the message I hear when I close my ears to God's Word. When I listen to the world, or permit my old sinful self to influence my life, I block God out. These temptations can easily lure me into saying, "Me first!" It is really an ancient battle that began when Adam and Eve fell into sin. Before sin, their whole existence was all about their Creator-God. Suddenly, in the aftermath of the fall, their perspectives became thoroughly distorted and *me* was the only thing that seemed to matter anymore.

Paul understood this. When he wrote to the Colossians, he refuted the heresy that said that human philosophy was needed to make up for God's inadequacies. When he wrote, "All things were created by him and for him" and that it is God who "in him all things hold together," it was a declaration that from the very beginning this world and our lives have always been only about God.

As I fight the temptation to make it all about me, I must return to my spiritual roots, to my baptism. It was there that God claimed me to be his. At that moment, when I was splashed by the water that was infused with God's love and Spirit, my life ceased to be about me. It was then that my purpose was defined. From that moment on, my life has been held together by him whose brokenness on the cross brought completeness to our lives.

So despite what I see, what I hear, and what I do, it really isn't about me. When Adam and Eve recovered from the initial shock of realizing it wasn't about them, God stepped in with a plan of salvation that allowed them to live life to his glory. Those are the same words we hear today. Remember your calling today. It is a calling from God to the place you are right now—a calling to be around the people you are with. It's about him who loved us enough to send his Son. If we know and remember that fact, we'll turn the question "It's not about me?" into a declaration: "It's not about me!" That declaration signals to all around us that the power of God lives in us.

He Is Our God; We Are His People

If we live, we live to the Lord; and if we die, we die to the Lord. So, whether we live or die, we belong to the Lord.
Romans 14:8

Over 20 years ago, my oldest son was in 4-year-old prekindergarten. The teacher invited the kids to have their parents come in and help in some way. At the time I was coaching varsity boys soccer. I arranged to bring five or six of my players to the school to do a demonstration and then work with the kids for a little while. When the time came, the teacher asked my son to introduce us. My son came over, took my hand, turned to the group, and simply said, "This is Daddy." For some reason I have always remembered that simple introduction as being just about the best introduction I could ever receive. Even though telling this story may embarrass my son a little, it is one of those moments that is very clear in my mind.

There was no doubt that day that I was his daddy and he was my son. Today my boys are often connected to me by people who say we look alike, sound alike, or even think alike. I'm glad to hear such comments. That kind of parental pride is a feeling that one treasures for life.

It is often said that teams reflect their coach, choirs reflect their director, or classes reflect their teacher. Could it also be said of us that we reflect our God?

This passage from Paul makes it clear that we belong to God. He is our God. He's not going to back down. He accepts us because he is our God, because he loves us, because he has forgiven us for Jesus' sake. But do we show that we are his people?

Through the things we say and do every day, are we taking his hand and proudly announcing him as Daddy? When God claimed us, through his Holy Spirit, he also gave us the power to boldly announce that we are his children.

Think about that today. What did you do in the last hour to boldly announce that you are his child? What in our classrooms says we are his children? What can you do to help your students grow in faith and confidence so that they too will boldly announce, "We are his people"?

If I begin to doubt God's sincerity, I merely need to remember the baptismal washing I received when I was a week old and the body and blood I received last week at the Communion rail. Those sacraments are as bold as any statement can be. By washing me in his love and forgiveness, God claims me and keeps me. He wants to be my God—a loving, caring, forgiving God. Do I have the same passion to be one of his people? That's where regular worship, reading his Word, and partaking of the sacrament come into play. They help revive that passion when it ebbs.

I pray that you and I continue to tap into the power of the Spirit in all we do so that our lives proclaim, "We are his people," today and every day. Invite the Spirit to turn your classroom into a place where everyone—teacher or student—proudly takes the hand of God and unashamedly announces, "He is my God, and I am his child."

General

Growing in the Lord

We pray this in order that you may live a life worthy of the Lord and may please him in every way: bearing fruit in every good work, growing in the knowledge of God, being strengthened with all power according to his glorious might so that you may have great endurance and patience, and joyfully giving thanks to the Father. *Colossians 1:10-12*

This week is homecoming at our school. The whole week is, by nature, hectic, frenetic, even chaotic at times. With dress-up days, the coronation, athletic events, a pep rally, a bonfire, and the dance, it seems as though it may never end. It also happens to be the end of our first six-week grading period, with all the angst and work for teachers and students that accompany that event. Taken together, and depending on your viewpoint, this week is either a symphony of joyous high school events or a cacophony of events determined to undermine learning. Of course we rejoice with the kids and hope they have fun. At the same time, we worry about some of them making the wrong choices related to drinking, drugs, and sexual activity.

It seems obvious to connect this theme to our calling as teachers. We are supposed to help our students grow in knowledge, in both the academic and spiritual realms. Yet for me, the real key to understanding this verse is the "bearing fruit" part.

I'm not much of a gardener; I throw a couple of tomato plants in the ground and hope they grow. But I do water them, fertilize them occasionally, and cover them when there are frost warnings. If I don't get decent fruit, it all seems to have been a waste.

Shouldn't we be looking for some fruit from our students? That's really how we know they're growing. Certainly, it's not going to happen without the help of the Spirit. But to be true to our calling as teachers, it's not enough just to inundate them with information; we need to give them opportunities to bear fruit.

It seems to me that homecoming and grading periods are just such times. We help our young people handle responsibility by giving it to them. We pray that they bear fruit during homecoming festivities. Whether it is during an athletic contest, at a dance, or with their dates and friends during the evening, these are opportunities for teachers and parents to give them a chance to bear fruit in their attitudes and actions.

And when they don't? Just like my tomatoes, I may need to water them a little more, fertilize them a little more, and even warn them about the frost. (Okay, I don't talk to my tomatoes, but you get the point.)

One other thing, did you notice how the passage says that people who grow in the Lord will be able to show more endurance and patience? I think that applies just as much to the teacher as it does to the student. As you grow in the Lord, you begin to realize that you do have patience and endurance during weeks like this. You also have potential for patience and endurance during those hectic times in your life outside of school. That's what growth is all about—understanding how to apply the knowledge you've acquired.

Finally, there's that little part in the text that talks about "giving thanks to the Father." Don't overlook that thought, even if you're just thanking him for getting you through this week. By sending his Son and through the power of his Spirit, the Father gives each one of us unlimited potential to grow. Take advantage of that in your own life. Recognize it. And give thanks for it.

Have a great week, growing in the Lord.

Homecoming

"But you, O mountains of Israel, will produce branches and fruit for my people Israel, for they will soon come home."
Ezekiel 36:8

Last week was homecoming week at our school. It's a time when graduates make their way back to memories of their youth. Many alumni, of various ages and from different parts of the country, return home to their alma mater. At our school, a couple of graduates from last year even made their way into the locker room after the game.

It's those recent graduates that I think most about every year. They seem oddly out of place. While the amount of time they've spent away from us is short, the distance they've traveled is great. It's as though they're saying to themselves, "Toto, I've got a feeling we're not in Kansas anymore."

I thought of that also when I recently made airplane reservations to have our son fly home from grad school for Thanksgiving and Christmas. As it should be, his life is moving on without his mother and me constantly at his side. Our lives and his are becoming less and less entwined. When he comes home, it is different, for all of us. Home is different. I tell that to seniors all the time. You can come back as often as you want, but something changes the minute you walk across that stage.

Our relationship with God can be eerily similar. When they ate of the fruit, Adam and Eve found how profoundly empty life without God is. Eden, *home* if you will, was not the same. Things looked different. Adam and Eve looked different, to themselves and to each other. Their world was different. They needed God to step in and provide a way to come home.

We go through the same process every day. Each day we awake is a reminder: it is a new day for us in Christ. Through our baptisms we are reminded that we die in Christ and rise in him each and every day. Yet, like Adam and Eve, it doesn't take us long to find a way to mess up our home with God. We sin, and soon things are different. We are scarred by guilt and devastated by the consequences of our sin. Our home with Christ is then inexorably changed.

And so it is with all those around us whom we are called to serve. They too are seeking a stable home. But guilty consciences keep getting in the way. For us, and for them, God's open arms are extended. He invites us home and prepares a regal place for us.

Being a poor grad student, our son probably couldn't have afforded to come home if we had not paid for the flight. I'm certain that I have no chance of getting back to my home with God without Christ intervening. His sacrifice on the cross has given me the opportunity to share in his death and his resurrection through my baptism. His payment in blood allows me to feel, for now, that I am already at home with him. One day that arrangement will become permanent—for the rest of eternity. "There's no place like home."

General

In Love, Helping One Another

Give us aid against the enemy, for the help of man is worthless. With God we will gain the victory, and he will trample down our enemies. Psalm 108:12,13

Yesterday, late in the afternoon, I was in my office, doing some work. A student came in and said I was needed in the locker room because a JV player had injured his ankle. I have to be honest; my first thoughts were not about how I could help but rather, "Where are the JV coaches, and why aren't they taking care of it?" Or maybe, "Why me? My day is done here!" Grudgingly, I went down to help. The JV coach just wanted another opinion. You guessed it: I was put out because I had to help.

My reality is that I could relate better, but I'm just not one of those people who gets joy out of helping others at the expense of my own time. I admire those individuals who truly go out of their way to help others with no thought as to how it might benefit themselves.

This psalm helps me understand that my help, when done out of the wrong motivation, is pretty useless. The words "with God" are important here. They could easily replace "in love" in this title. With God's Holy Spirit alive in me, I will help others . . . and selfless love will be my true motivation for doing so.

It's a temptation to say that as a church worker, I'm exempt from going out of my way to help others. That kind of thinking gets me back to this idea that it's me who's providing the impetus and power to help others.

I really need to remind myself that God gives me the power and the victory over selfishness and laziness.

Helping one another should be a joy. It should be a joy because our lives in Christ are a joy. I'm not talking about nothing-bad-ever-happens-because-God-loves-me joy, but real, true, down-to-my-soul joy. It's the kind of joy that is mine because God's love and forgiveness enable me to see life from a whole new perspective. That new perspective views helping others as a benefit and a blessing of having life in Christ, not as a way to gain life in Christ.

People expect a lot from church workers. They have a right to have such high expectations. We've said that our relationship with God means so much to us that we want to make it a part of everything we do in life, our job included. But those expectations can easily turn into demands. That's when I need to remember, again, that on my own I'm worthless. But with God I truly can help others in an unselfish way, even if they may not always want my help.

For now I need to concentrate on using the power of God to help the people around me. With his help, we will gain the victory.

Your Will, Not Mine, O Lord

Going a little farther, he fell with his face to the ground and prayed, "My Father, if it is possible, may this cup be taken from me. Yet not as I will, but as you will." Matthew 26:39

On Saturday, at my son's football game, the opposing team ran several passing plays and scored with only 33 seconds left in the game. This may not sound like much, but they were already winning 41-6 when this happened. I was beside myself with anger and with questions about the sportsmanship of the opposing team.

Then last night, the speaker at our National Honor Society induction spoke briefly about how students should strive to be the person that Christ wants them to be, not who their parents or their teachers or their friends want them to be. Those words made me reflect on Saturday's events. Did the opposing coach make decisions based on what he thought his players or the fans or his school wanted? Or did he make decisions based on his own integrity? Or on the other side of the coin were my reactions based on what I wanted for my son and his team or just on my opinion about what is good sportsmanship?

As an educator, I find that I often have preconceived little boxes I want my students to fit into. I have an idea of what they should be able to do. And I feel like my goals for them are the best ones for them. After all, I always have their best interests in mind, and I surely know better than they do about what's good for them.

As a parent, I foresee great futures for my sons—futures that fit into my world of what's important.

After all, I always have their best interests at heart, and surely I know better than they do about what's good for them!

As a husband, I have great plans for my wife's and my life together as a couple. The plans I have revolve around what I think is best. After all, I am the husband, and I am always thinking about our best interests. And I know better that anyone about what's good for us!

As an individual, I have great plans for my life. I try to manipulate my life and situations to fit into my plans. After all, I have only my own best interests in mind, and who else would know what's good for me?

And then it hits me right between the eyes: "Your will, not mine, O Lord." I have to confess that I'm constantly trying to make the people around me do what I want them to do. I force people into boxes that I've created, trying to get them to see things my way. I agonize when the lives of people I love and care about don't work out according to *my* plans. What I don't get is that it's not supposed to be my will that matters but God's.

Notice in the passage that Christ goes "a little farther" and then prays those words. I think that's what I need to do when I find myself trying to impose my will over others; I need to step away from the pressures of everyday life. I need to go a little farther and ask God to forgive my selfishness and to open my eyes to the idea of being what he wants me to be. After all, he always does have my best interests in mind, and surely God does know better than I do about what's good for me.

Celebrating the Reformation

I am not ashamed of the gospel, because it is the power of God for the salvation of everyone who believes: first for the Jew, then for the Gentile. For in the gospel a righteousness from God is revealed, a righteousness that is by faith from first to last, just as it is written: "The righteous will live by faith." Romans 1:16,17

This Sunday our school is hosting a Reformation Day celebration. When I was a youngster, an annual Reformation Day Rally was held in the auditorium in downtown Milwaukee. Thousands of people attended each year. And none of them worried if his or her favorite football team was playing at the same time.

It seems to me that being a Lutheran Christian means celebrating God's great love and forgiveness. His love is evident to us through his Word and the sacraments. *Grace alone, faith alone,* and *Scripture alone* were the words that Luther used to describe the foundation of his faith. That is what our schools and churches must proclaim in order to be called Lutheran. The message of God's grace (the undeserved love of God and his forgiveness) that is ours through faith is all we need to hear. And we need to hear it, not only on Reformation Day but every day.

The number of people who celebrate Reformation Day is not as important as how many people embrace God's love. The Word of God and the sacraments give us God's love all the time. Have you listened to that Word today? Have you spoken that Word to others? Have you remembered your baptism or thought about the last time you received the Lord's Supper? If so, Reformation Day is happening for you. And you can celebrate that any time of the year.

> Rejoice therefore that through his Son
> Your God with you is now at one.
> He took on human flesh and bone,
> And you, his brothers, are God's own.
>
> God came to share himself with you;
> Your sin and death he overthrew.
> The foe may send his fiery dart,
> Your friend, God's Son, will shield your heart.
>
> He never will abandon you.
> Trust King, Immanuel the True.
> Yield not to any evil might.
> Walk in the Christ Child's saving light.
>
> Then in the end you will prevail;
> God's friends and brothers cannot fail.
> In praise to God then raise your voice,
> Prepare forever to rejoice!
>
> *Martin Luther*

General

A Caring, Christian Community

[Isaac blessed Jacob and said,] *"May God Almighty bless you and make you fruitful and increase your numbers until you become a community of peoples." Genesis 28:3*

I bet you didn't know that the word *community* is found in the Old Testament 84 times and only once in the New Testament. The discrepancy probably has something to do with the sense of community that was evident in the Jewish culture. Their ethnic, cultural, religious, and geographical connections helped create the idea of community. They had bonds that were strengthened by their faith, but those bonds were also present for other reasons apart from their religion. However, as the New Testament church grew, many of these other community connections lessened or disappeared.

The same may be said of many of our congregations and schools. It is possible that we see members of our congregation only at worship. Our members are so spread out that a notion of community doesn't always exist. Our schools have students from many diverse backgrounds. Outside of school, community is hard to develop.

So how do we begin to create a *community* atmosphere?

The title of this devotion gives us the answer. First, we must be in Christ. This sounds simple. In reality, it is a challenge. Sure, we have chapels, morning and afternoon prayers, and religion classes. But being in Christ means letting Christ be in us. We have to open our lives to the potential that is ours when Christ, through God's Spirit and the power of the gospel, takes hold of our lives. When we understand our baptismal calling, we understand that we have Christ in us and that we are in Christ. As teaching staff, we have the responsibility to model this for the young people in our care. We have been called to this place to do just that.

Second, we need to strive to be a caring community. Caring for someone means more than a cursory *How are you?* Christ cared by spending time with those for whom he cared, by coming to earth and living among those for whom he would later die. Taking time to talk to coworkers and students helps send the message that we care. Christ cared by forgiving. Christ cared by admonishing. Most important, Christ cared by finding a way to love all of us, even as sinners. Can we find a way to love everyone in our community?

Caring for someone is a very personal matter. Elementary schools, secondary schools, and colleges often quote former students as saying that they felt like the teachers in that school really cared for them. That's nice. But we've been called to create a caring community that is in Christ. Don't forget that. Demand that of yourself. Hold yourself to that standard. Such caring will be reflected in *how* you care for others. In the caring things you say and do for your students, you will let them see Jesus living in your life. In caring for them, you will also be telling them about Jesus and his great love for them.

Pray that your school shows evidence of being in Christ by the caring attitudes had by all who are part of your community.

General

Alive in God's Promise

So do not throw away your confidence; it will be richly rewarded. You need to persevere so that when you have done the will of God, you will receive what he has promised. But we are not of those who shrink back and are destroyed, but of those who believe and are saved.
Hebrews 10:35,36,39

During the first year that I was teaching at Martin Luther High School, the theme for the year was "Alive in God's Promise." It was a great theme because everything seemed alive to me. It was a different city, a different school, different coworkers, all the things that go with accepting a call to a new setting. Additionally, my wife was expecting our first child, and because this was in the "old" days, we didn't know the gender ahead of time. I was young, full of brash confidence. I would never have thought of shrinking back; life was full speed ahead.

Fast forward to now. I don't always feel so alive. Persevering seems more like "putting up with" or "putting in my time." I'm more willing to shrink back rather than to think about the effort it will take to step up to a new challenge. Many days it seems to be a real challenge to be true to my calling as an educator. Some days I wonder if I haven't put in enough time already.

At this point it would be easy to lapse into a self-pitying, introspective essay about how we change through life, but I don't think that's what this is about. To be alive in God's promise is to be filled with the passion and excitement that accompanies our joy in being a child of God. Sometimes those of us who have been lifelong Christians are lulled into a *safe* faith—one that is shrinking without us knowing it.

Did you ever try out for something? How did you feel when you saw your name on the list? For me there always was a sense of exhilaration. When I made that team or got that part, I was brimming with confidence, sure that I could do the job, alive with excitement. Life as a Christian should be filled with that same exhilaration.

Luther suggests we make the sign of the cross in the morning as a reminder of our baptisms—a reminder, if you will, of when God made us spiritually alive and brought us into his family of believers.

God sees a lot of promise in us. Through Word and sacrament, his Spirit brings us to life and causes us to grow in faith rather than shrink. Alive in faith, we are able to fulfill the promise God sees in us. We can persevere, be confident, and do the job he has planned for us. Striving to do his will means being alive in God's promise.

Now look at your students. What can you do to help them be alive in God's promise? And how can you help them fulfill the promise God has in store for their lives?

Being alive in God's promise is all about using the power of faith to have a living and vibrant relationship with God. When that relationship is alive, our lives take on a different tone. Instead of dwelling on those moments of indecision and doubt, our confidence level is sky high, knowing that new life is ours through Christ. Because he lives, so can we.

General

It's Only a Game

Whatever you do, work at it with all your heart, as working for the Lord, not for men. *Colossians 3:23*

If you have never been part of a team, these thoughts from the letter to the Colossians may be a little hard to relate to. After watching my son's college football team lose their last game of the season (in overtime no less) and watching these young men deal with their emotions, it got me thinking about people who say things like "What's the big deal? It's only a game!" I remember a high school game of my own where otherwise tough high school guys cried in the locker room after losing a 21-20 game. I've been a coach of many teams—both girls' and boys' teams—whose members unashamedly shed tears after a game. I've shed a few of my own as a coach. And now I've seen college guys shed tears.

Unless you've been part of something where you put your emotions, your body, or your intellect into the pursuit of excellence, you can't fully appreciate these emotions. But I also believe that many of these emotions are triggered by feelings for, and about, the other players involved, not feelings about the losing experience itself. It comes down to the passion for what one is trying to accomplish and the ability to turn that passion into something tangible.

That kind of passion was displayed in the Bible too. How about a starting lineup of Bible greats? Don't tell me you wouldn't want David on your side, or Joseph, Elijah, or Peter. How about Luke as the team physician? Don't forget about Samson, Daniel, Gideon, Joshua, John the Baptist, and Moses. This team could be co-ed. I don't have a problem with Deborah, Hannah, or Jael being on the team. All of these are examples of people who turned their passion for God into action. And if you think Jesus wasn't passionate, then your view of him is a lot different from mine. I see Jesus as a person who wanted to win—all the time. His desire to defeat sin led him to the cross. Along the way, there were tears and times when he needed to be by himself. And there were times when he needed the support of his teammates.

Perhaps you're not passionate about athletics. Maybe you're more passionate about music, your family, or your job. The question we all need to ask ourselves is, *How passionate are we about our faith?* The thing that set those great Bible personalities apart from others was their overwhelming passion for God and their relationship with him.

I am frequently guilty of failing to display that kind of passion as a regular part of my life. I let the trials and tribulations of everyday life interfere with that passion. I fail to fully use the talents I've been given. It's much like an athlete letting the discomfort of minor injuries or the apparent lack of commitment by teammates get in the way of his or her passion for playing the game.

To become passionate about our faith is not out of the question. God has graciously provided the framework and the power for us—we need to integrate both into our lives.

Perhaps some of you know, as I do, that terrible feeling in the pit of your stomach that comes from some disappointment over a loss. It sticks with you for days; often it only goes away with time. Most likely there are no words of consolation that can take away the bitterness of defeat, the sting of disappointment, or the sorrow of expectations unmet. The truly passionate person bounces back. Through faith and hope, the passionate participant picks himself or herself up and tries again.

Our faith-life isn't a game; it is so much more than that. It isn't just some nice-sounding words and a weekly visit to worship. Our lives as Christians are something to be passionate about. Pray for that passion in your life.

I'll never get used to losing. It just hurts too much. I pray I never get used to the pain of sin and guilt either. It hurts too much. What I want to get used to, with God's help, is a passion for my Savior. I want to have a passion for him that eclipses the setbacks of life and allows me to experience a joy that knows no bounds. I want to be passionate about his great and passionate love for me.

General

Hope Alive

Be joyful in hope. . . . May the God of hope fill you with all joy and peace as you trust in him, so that you may overflow with hope by the power of the Holy Spirit. Romans 12:12; 15:13

When I coached basketball, I used to tell players that they should shoot a free throw as though they knew it was going to go in, not as though they wished it would go in. I also felt that we needed to prepare for every game *believing* we would win, not just wanting to win. Truth is, there were many times I was just wishing because I didn't believe we really could win.

How about your personal life? For what are you hoping? That the marriage problems get worked out? That you don't have to put up with a certain kid in your class next year? That the medicine works? That nothing else breaks down in your home or car? Or is it something more along the lines of hoping for a special time with your family or a special present at Christmas?

Whatever you hope for, do it joyfully. Live a life that is filled with hope rather than disappointment.

But that's really hard to do, isn't it? It seems like all the people I know (myself included) lapse into the trap of dwelling on disappointments. We allow ourselves to get stuck on the harsh realities of life rather than live in joyful hope.

What makes a Christian's hope different is that our hope is built on a tangible reality. The reality of Christ's death and resurrection makes our hope far better than an idle wish or a wild-eyed stab in the dark.

Our hope for a better life, now and in eternity, is based on the reality of the Word made flesh: Christ.

Our hope becomes alive in us because of the gift of the Spirit, which is ours through Baptism. When our sinful flesh is drowned in the waters of life, our hope comes alive in us.

Back to those free throws. When you've shot enough free throws and have practiced them so that you consistently make them, hope becomes reality. When you've won enough games, you no longer hope to win, but you really do believe you'll win.

Our hope for a beautiful, everlasting life with Christ will also be a reality—a dream fulfilled. Until then we have a hope that rests in the sure promises of a God who has never once let us down in disappointment. That hope is the supreme reality of our lives.

Take a good look at the way you interact with others, including the young people in your classroom. Are you alive in the hope that is ours in Christ or are you shuffling through another day burdened by the realities of life? If you're having trouble with that concept, check back to the words of the apostle Paul. Start with trust in God and his promises to you. Those are the sure things! God's promises are as real as real can get. See your life as one of hope in a sure thing. Be alive in your calling as a child of God. You know God's love and the hope it generates within you. Be alive in that hope.

General

Blinded by My Vision

Taste and see that the LORD is good; blessed is the man who takes refuge in him. Psalm 34:8

[Jesus] said, "The knowledge of the secrets of the kingdom of God has been given to you, but to others I speak in parables, so that, 'though seeing, they may not see; though hearing, they may not understand.'" Luke 8:10

If I am remembering correctly, I was in the second grade when I had a case of the German measles. Back in the day before MMR shots, you got to stay home for two weeks, had all your stuff sent home, and didn't think it was all that bad to be sick. However, the measles did affect my eyesight, and I've worn glasses or contacts ever since.

So, anyhow, the other day I was visiting my optometrist, getting an exam, and figuring out how large a loan I was going to need to get new glasses and contacts. At one point I was sitting in the waiting area without contacts in or glasses on when I started thinking (which, for me, is always dangerous). Because I wear my contacts or glasses for all but 5 minutes every day, I tend to forget how poor my eyesight really is. I go through life quite unaware of my vision problem.

It's easy to do that in one's faith-life as well. We take our status as forgiven children of God for granted. I'm guilty of this all the time. I sometimes have myself convinced that I live life without sin. I go through life ignorant of how close I am to stepping off a precipice or into a wall. The real danger is that I fail to see how tainted by sin I really am. When that happens, I may

45

try and live outside of God's grace and love—to *go it alone*. Cloudy *spiritual* vision is far more perilous than if I try going through a day without devices to correct my poor physical vision. In that frame of mind, I can bring real spiritual harm to myself—and quite possibly others.

There's great comfort in knowing that my lenses on life, through the grace of God, have been corrected. I can see the problems—the sin. God's Word makes my life of sin shamefully clear. His law puts my sin into a focus so clear that it is painful to look at and admit. Yet I am most thankful to have such an excellent view of my life of sin. What I see clearly is my own hopelessly sinful condition and my desperation to find someone who can save me.

But with the corrected vision of God's Word, I also see that God has taken up my cause and washed me clean. Most devotions dealing with vision talk about our eyes being opened to see our sins and the need for God. Adam and Eve had their eyes opened in the Garden of Eden and saw their woeful state. But it was really the promise of a Savior that restored them to perfect vision. In that promise their flawed view of their Creator was restored. They may have been tempted to try to clear things up on their own. I know I am. It's like trying to take care of my vision problems on my own. I'd probably keep the same glasses for the rest of my life, ignoring the fact that I can't see as well as I once could. But God, in his love for me, stands ready to correct my vision every day, showing me my sin and my great need for the Savior. With that corrected spiritual vision, he leads me to see the way to eternal life with him. What a sight for sore eyes! Jesus, the beautiful Savior, is a vision to behold!

One day our bodies will be transformed in the glory of heaven—no need then for these glasses or contacts. Our spiritual vision will be cleared up too. Along with Adam and Eve, our spiritual vision will be 20/20. It won't be blurred by sins or temptations. The sights we will see then will be gloriously good and perfect.

A Cloudy Thanksgiving

Therefore, since we are surrounded by such a great cloud of witnesses, let us throw off everything that hinders and the sin that so easily entangles, and let us run with perseverance the race marked out for us. Hebrews 12:1

Have you ever noticed that it's always cloudy on Thanksgiving Day? Thanksgiving has always been one of my favorite holidays, clouds and all. It's a time of reflection. Let me share some reflections I'm having at this point in my life.

Walter, Flora, Martin J., LoNella, Martin W., Carol, Mark, Kristi, Susan, Bill, Elsa, Ruth, George. These are a few of the "great cloud" of witnesses in my life. Grandparents, parents, uncles, aunts, in-laws, all those relatives that were living lives of faith before I came around. From early on, they helped prepare me for my life's "race," modeling godly perseverance, courage, tenderness, compassion, generosity, humility. Some have gone ahead and are with God; others remain my guides for wherever life leads me.

Jean, Andrew, Jason. My wife and sons—other parts of the cloud. They constantly model God's love in their lives. Through their forgiveness for the times when I have failed, through their examples of caring for others, through their personal relationships with God, they lift me up.

Sarah, Mike, Tim, Jon, Michael, Karen, Ron, Meaghan. Other parts of my cloud bank. Relatives who probably don't even know how many times I have admired their strength of faith. Their words and actions build me up when I experience adversity.

Elsie, Emma, Erhardt, George, Don, Dave, Ralph, Roger, Gene, Richard, Tom, Alfred, Ken. From kindergarten through college and beyond, my cloud has been filled with godly teachers who have helped bolster my relationship with God through their teachings of his law and gospel. In and out of the classroom, they have helped prepare me for my life.

Roger, Gloria, Jim, Dave, Roman, Carl, Phil, Paul, Craig, Gary, Gene, Fred, Karen, Rollie, Curt, Linda, Becki, Tim, Marianne, and many more. From student teaching through today, God has blessed me with a protective, caring cloud of coworkers who remind me that it is possible to throw off all things that entangle, that it is possible to persevere, that it is possible to run the race. The way they treat me is a daily reminder of God's love and grace in my life. What a joy it is to be in a vocation that is also a ministry!

Heather, Dana, Sarah, Kyle, Tim, Dave, Katie, Angela, Jill, Justin, Hope, Kristin, Melissa, Jenny, Josh, Ric, Dan, Mike, Ashley, and many more. This part of the cloud is made up of all the many students I've known. They have shown me that faith in God can occur at any age. These young people frequently have a clearer sense of the races they are running than I do of my own. At times I feel God has put me into their lives, while in reality it is often the other way around. The times they have lifted me up are probably unknown to them, but they are remembered by me.

There are many others: *neighbors, friends, pastors, and my own classmates*—other wisps of my cloud of witnesses. Through all of these people, God continues to shower me with his love and care. They provide me strength when I need to be encouraged in my race.

They have pointed out my flaws and sins, even while they were anxious to guide me back to God. They have forgiven me and lifted me up when I was disappointed in myself. And empowered by the Holy Spirit, they have kept me on the course marked out for me.

This is why my Thanksgiving is always cloudy. God has surrounded me not only with his love but with a great cloud of witnesses. I pray that you too can fill in the names within your cloud and feel the power of God alive in your surrounding cloud of witnesses.

Saying "Thank You" Too Much

So then, just as you received Christ Jesus as Lord, continue to live in him, rooted and built up in him, strengthened in the faith as you were taught, and overflowing with thankfulness. See to it that no one takes you captive through hollow and deceptive philosophy, which depends on human tradition and the basic principles of this world rather than on Christ. *Colossians 2:6-8*

Recently I read an article entitled "Do we say 'thank you' too much?" The gist was that people no longer say, "You're welcome." According to the article, we're more likely to return a "thank you" with something like "No, thank *you*." Too many people, the article said, use the phrase "you're welcome" in a condescending manner or just simply think it's assumed.

Maybe the real problem is that we have so many phrases in our lives that have become just that—phrases. They have no real meaning because we use them so thoughtlessly. *I'm sorry, How are you? Nice to meet you, Let me know if there's anything I can do,* and even *I love you* can easily become just words. And how about the Lord's Prayer? or the words of confession during worship? They can easily become words we merely parrot as well.

Paul recognized this problem when he was writing to the Colossians. Apparently some people were spending a lot of time in theological discourse without making the transition to everyday life. Paul's point was to get out there and live as a follower of Jesus.

Thanksgiving is at the heart of a godly life. The good news makes us appreciate God's undeserved love and forgiveness. Words like *forgiveness* and *grace* can never be allowed to become meaningless throwaways. Our eternity rests on them.

For those of us who are teachers or parents, it's easy to talk about doctrine and much harder to let the Spirit control our lives. It's easy to say "I'm sorry" or "I love you" and much harder to show it. God, through his Son, really shows us that he means what he says. When God says, "I love you," he gives us his Son as a sacrifice to take our punishment for us.

Maybe we do say thank you too much and then fail to show it enough. To those around you whom you love—family, students, coworkers—*show* them you love them, don't just say it. Live the love and forgiveness God has shown you.

When we say thank you to God, he says, "You're welcome" by welcoming us into his loving arms and gently wiping away our tears caused by guilt. He says, "You're welcome" and then invites us to be surrounded by his love—forever.

Now that's something for which we can never say thank you too much.

In the Light of His Love

God saw that the light was good, and he separated the light from the darkness. *Genesis 1:4*

[John the Baptist] himself was not the light; he came only as a witness to the light. The true light that gives light to every man was coming into the world. *John 1:8,9*

As I sit here, staring out my window on a drizzly November day with its forlorn gray clouds, I'm struck by how easy it is to let weather affect my mood. I feel like I'm getting sleepier as the day goes on. On the other hand, when my screen saver kicks in, my eyes are massaged with a luxurious blend of blues and greens that represent the best photo of an idyllic tropical island. My spirits are lifted, if only for a brief moment, as I imagine being bathed in the warmth and light of this breathtaking oasis.

I can completely understand why people go to tanning salons. It's not so much for the tanning but to insulate themselves from the nasty weather outside. That's what I want in my life too. I want to bottle up the good days and use that joy to disperse the melancholy feelings that seep into my being on the bleaker days.

This theme speaks to that possibility. While light is a common theme of devotions and sermons, I see these words a little differently. God's love for me, in the person of his Son, radiates a light that encompasses every part of me. It's like the follow spot of some stage production. You know, the kind that follows the performer wherever he or she goes. God's love follows me wherever I go and whatever I do. His light is always shining on me. It's not like the kind of spotlight used at a premiere. That light seems to try to pierce the darkness. I say "try" because eventually the light dissipates and is swallowed up by the sheer volume of darkness it seeks to penetrate.

That's what would happen to me if I tried to be my own light. I simply can't pierce the darkness and gloom of a life that's been infected with sin. However, when I allow myself to be the object of God's love and to be engulfed in his light, then I can see through the darkness. Then I truly am surrounded by the light of his love, and I am forgiven for those times when I have tried to depend on my own power source, which is never sufficient.

Most parents have experienced a time when their child has said something like "I just need a hug!" Or maybe you remember a time when you felt that way. It's easy to feel that way in a world that eats away at our confidences and creates more concerns than calms. That's when we need to return to the light of his love.

These are not new ideas. The Advent season reflects a longing for the coming of God's precious Light to the world. We hear it in this hymn stanza:

> Oh, come, O Dayspring from on high,
> And cheer us by your drawing nigh;
> Disperse the gloomy clouds of night,
> And death's dark shadows put to flight.
>
> *Latin Hymn*

What makes your life "gloomy"? Not sure about the future? Stay in the Light. Not sure about your relationships? Stay in the Light. Feeling like there is more failure than success in your life? Stay in the Light. Things not working out the way you wanted them to? Stay in the Light. Feeling out of control? Stay in the Light. Just plain afraid? Stay in the Light. Need a hug? Stay in the Light!

The Light of God's love is ours for keeps. The weather outside can change, but through his Spirit, we can stay in the Light forever.

Advent

A Mighty Fortress Lying in a Manger

God is our refuge and strength, an ever-present help in trouble. The Lord Almighty is with us; the God of Jacob is our fortress. *Psalm 46:1,7*

While they were there, the time came for the baby to be born, and she gave birth to her firstborn, a son. She wrapped him in cloths and placed him in a manger, because there was no room for them in the inn. *Luke 2:6,7*

About 15 years ago we bought a Christmas recording that included an instrumental version of "A Mighty Fortress," the great Reformation hymn. The odd thing about this recording was that the melody eventually gave way to a familiar Christmas carol. That same Christmas was a particularily stressful one. My wife was in the hospital on Christmas Eve. There was a certain tenseness in the air as we were only weeks away from the first Gulf War.

I also recall that I did a chapel service during January of that year in which I took many of the words from the stanzas of "A Mighty Fortress" and applied them to certain events in my life. It began to make perfect sense to me why Luther's great Reformation anthem belonged on that recording with that Christmas song. Just the other day we played the recording again, and it occurred to me that on that Christmas I had truly needed to know that a Mighty Fortress had come to be in Bethlehem's manger.

While we sing "What Child Is This" and "Away in a Manger," we are often wrapped up in the beauty and serenity of Christmas. In many ways I think we want to forget about the horror of Good Friday because it brings us face-to-face with Christ's death and our part in it. The perfect antidote is to imagine the peaceful manger where an infant lay, who, as the carol says, "No crying he makes." In some ways we've sanitized Christmas in order to forget about the guilt, the sin, and the death that sin brings upon us. None of those fit into our picture of the perfect Christmas. We'd prefer to dream of a white Christmas to cover up a bleak and ugly earth.

The beauty of Christmas is important and should be celebrated in song and words. But the reality of Christmas is that it was necessary because of our sin. The reality of Christmas is that the little baby born in the stable is the *mighty fortress* we need and depend on. That little baby is the "valiant one," whom God himself chose in eternity to take up the fight for us. That little baby allows us to stare death in the face and "tremble not." That little baby gives us the courage to "fear no ill." In him the victory is won.

"The kingdom's ours forever" because of that baby. To celebrate the birth without remembering the death and resurrection is to miss the point entirely.

There will be much joy and much celebration this Christmas season. There will also be sadness intermingled as feelings are hurt, loved ones are missed, and the reverberations of sin and selfishness surround us. But *joy to the world, a mighty fortress is come!*

Advent

I Can Wait for Christmas

We know that the whole creation has been groaning as in the pains of childbirth right up to the present time. Not only so, but we ourselves, who have the firstfruits of the Spirit, groan inwardly as we wait eagerly for our adoption as sons, the redemption of our bodies. For in this hope we were saved. But hope that is seen is no hope at all. Who hopes for what he already has? But if we hope for what we do not yet have, we wait for it patiently. In the same way, the Spirit helps us in our weakness. We do not know what we ought to pray for, but the Spirit himself intercedes for us with groans that words cannot express. And he who searches our hearts knows the mind of the Spirit, because the Spirit intercedes for the saints in accordance with God's will. And we know that in all things God works for the good of those who love him, who have been called according to his purpose. *Romans 8:22-28*

I have a confession to make: I'm not breathlessly waiting for the end of the world. Truth be told, I kind of like my life here on earth. Heaven sounds great and all, but despite a lot of little aggravations, I wake up on earth every day confident of God's love for me. Perhaps living after-the-fact of the first Christmas has somehow lessened my anticipation of the second coming.

I've always admired the people who lived before Christ. From Adam and Eve to Zechariah and Elizabeth, God's people were fortified in their faith by a promise. They really couldn't do much but wait. We know the end of the story; they believed the story would end the way God told them it would. The waiting was part of God's plan. They trusted that waiting patiently for God to fulfill his promises would strengthen them in their faith.

I very seldom see the benefits of waiting. Just yesterday I was slowed down while driving behind someone who had a different interpretation of the speed limit than I did. At the next stoplight, I said a little prayer for patience, which turned into a prayer about some other things in my life. As I drove away, I came to the conclusion that waiting is good.

That's what Paul is telling the Romans. Waiting gives God a chance to work with us some more. He's obviously in no hurry. He sees the whole plan and even sends us his Spirit to encourage us in our waiting. It is when we become impatient with God that God's Spirit is most needed. In our sinful and frail condition as human beings, we are forced to look again with confidence to Christ and his salvation.

There are many times in life we say we can't wait. Four-year-olds can't wait for kindergarten, eighth graders for high school, high schoolers for college, engaged couples for marriage. We wait for our children to be born, and then we wait for them to leave home. We wait for our kids to get married, and then we wait for them to have grandchildren. We wait to have a job, and then we wait for retirement. It is those waiting times when we grow and are made ready for the next steps in our lives. In our patient times of waiting, God works to strengthen us.

Sometimes our students don't understand why certain classes are required. In the same way we may question God about why certain things happen in life—a death, an illness, the loss of a good job, an argument. That is why we must believe Paul when he tells us that God knows us better than we know ourselves—that in love he works out every detail of our lives for our own good.

That's what the message of Advent is about: waiting, trusting that God will make good on all of his promises. God makes us wait because we're not ready. He still has a few more things to accomplish in us.

God's Secret: Christ Is in You

We speak of God's secret wisdom, a wisdom that has been hidden and that God destined for our glory before time began. None of the rulers of this age understood it, for if they had, they would not have crucified the Lord of glory. However, as it is written: "No eye has seen, no ear has heard, no mind has conceived what God has prepared for those who love him"—but God has revealed it to us by his Spirit. 1 Corinthians 2:7-10

At this time of the year, it's not unusual to hear children exclaim, "I just can't wait for Christmas!" No matter the reason, waiting is really hard. Even adults have difficulty learning to wait. Whether we're anticipating good or bad events, it's tough because we just don't know what's going to happen.

Advent is a time when we are to practice waiting. During this time of waiting, we are to become prepared. We are preparing for an event that we already know about. But often it's not easy to do that. We have better plans; we want to fit God's plan into our timetable. We think we already know the answer to how it's going to turn out. So why wait? It's a problem with which God's people have always struggled.

Old Testament people, Mary and Joseph, the disciples, the early church, and God's people throughout the centuries have sought answers about Christ's coming, for the first time or for the second. Patience often has grown thin. We are alike. We want answers now—we want to see evidence of Christ now—we want God's secret revealed now!

Let's be honest, many times we place God into the same category as the rest of the people in our lives. We treat God in the same way we treat our students (Why don't they understand what I'm teaching?) or our coworkers (Why won't they listen to me?) or the folks in the office (What is the administration waiting for?) or our loved ones (Why don't they see it my way?). We question the Lord's timing and his plans for our lives. It's almost as if we think we deserve answers.

One of the beautiful things about the season of Advent is that it teaches us patience. It should also remind us to confess that we don't deserve the wonderful gifts promised to us by God, much less the knowledge of how and when these gifts will be delivered into our lives. It should help us develop an appreciation for the time of preparation, not just the revelation.

The best news about this season of patient waiting is that we already have access to God's secret. His greatest gift to us, his love made manifest in his Son, is ours through the gift of his Spirit to us in our baptisms. We have the inside scoop on God's plans. Because of our baptisms, Christ is already living in us.

Too often our preoccupation with things of the world obscures the wisdom of God's secret. The prophet Isaiah said it first and Paul quoted him, "No eye has seen, no ear has heard, no mind has conceived what God has prepared for those who love him" (Isaiah 64:4; 1 Corinthians 2:9). It's a plan for each of us. First, we learn to wait and trust. Second, we learn that what God has in mind for us is so grand, we cannot comprehend it. Finally, we live in the joy of knowing God's secret, because he is already a part of every moment and phase of our lives.

In this Advent season, spend some time dwelling on the preparing and the waiting—God will take care of the rest.

Advent

Open Our Eyes, Lord

When he was at the table with them, he took bread, gave thanks, broke it and began to give it to them. Then their eyes were opened and they recognized him. Luke 24:30,31

People who smoke. Guys with tongue studs. People who have offensive bumper stickers on their cars. Football players who celebrate after every play. These are just a few of the things that cause me to prejudge people. I struggle with this a lot. They're probably wonderful people. I just don't see it. Too many times I've closed my eyes, and my heart, to people rather than try to look past their outward appearances. I know I've unfairly judged students, fellow faculty, neighbors, and people sitting in the next pew at church. I suppose it's inevitable that my sinful nature incites this type of behavior in me, but I'm not happy about it. I know better, and I need to work at it.

I probably would have judged Mary and Joseph by their shabby clothes and lack of money, banishing them to some dingy stable. I would have ignored the shepherds as some smelly field hands. I would have missed the significance of the child in the manger because I would have seen nothing more than a useless infant wrapped in rags and lying in a feed box with a bunch of mangy animals milling about nearby.

I've convinced myself that my view of the world is the right one, as if I am God. In this regard, I'm no better than Herod, the chief priests, or the Pharisees in the way they treated Christ.

We each need to learn this about ourselves: We are reflections of our own sinful nature, and we treat others accordingly. When that lesson finally sinks in and we begin to recognize that we need a better view—God's view—of how things really are, it's time for some *good news.* And isn't that what Christmas is all about . . . good news?

Part of the good news is that my eyes can be opened. God has provided me with some clarity for how I see others around me. He opens my eyes to see first what Jesus has done for me and then to see how I am to be more like him in the way that I treat other people.

We have to wonder at how the eyes of those two disciples on the road to Emmaus were opened. They had spent the afternoon together with Jesus, reflected on the Old Testament teachings, broken bread with him.

Sooner or later it dawns on us that Jesus comes to us in ways that are not really so different. We can hear his Word in worship, talk with him in prayer, and break bread with him in the Lord's Supper. But notice that the Scripture tells us that their eyes "were opened"; they did not open their eyes themselves.

God's Holy Spirit will open our eyes as well. As we listen to God speak to us in his Holy Word, we begin to see the truth about ourselves—our faults and sins, our selfish natures. That view is truly disturbing. But when God opens our eyes to see the whole picture, we see Jesus and his great love for us. Then, like those two disciples who met Jesus on the road to Emmaus, our hearts also burn with the good news of the gospel.

In this Advent season, remember to ask God to forgive you for so often missing the great view he wants you to see. Pray that he will open your eyes to a whole new view of the world . . . as he sees it.

Advent

Don't Touch That Contrast Button!

Stop doing wrong, learn to do right! Seek justice, encourage the oppressed. Defend the cause of the fatherless, plead the case of the widow. "Come now, let us reason together," says the LORD. "Though your sins are like scarlet, they shall be as white as snow; though they are red as crimson, they shall be like wool." *Isaiah 1:16-18*

As we come to the end of the third week of Advent, the week of the pink candle, we are reminded that this is the joy week of Advent. My wife, who teaches kindergarten, was telling me how excited her kids were last week as they looked forward to lighting that pink candle. It was true joy and excitement as they learned the wonders of Advent leading up to Christmas. They could hardly wait to see that candle lit again in church during the weekend and again in their classroom on Monday.

Last week our school community attended the funeral of one of our students who was killed in an automobile accident. There wasn't much joy apparent during the service. There were lots of tears and hugs and whispered words as young and old alike came to grips with the reality of death—within a season that is about the anticipation of a birth. The unbridled joy of five-year-olds was in sharp contrast to the subdued and somber atmosphere of worshipers saying their earthly good-byes to a friend and student.

Think of the contrasts in your own life. Perhaps it is the darkness of sin eclipsed by the forgiveness of baptism or the sadness that comes with the death of a loved one that is replaced by the joy we find in the sure confidence of life everlasting with our Lord.

The contrast that Isaiah speaks of when he says that our scarlet sins will be turned as white as snow is a contrast that gives meaning to our lives. Because of this promise, God provides each of us with a brightly burning, pink joy candle during each day and every season. It is this loving promise that should propel us to follow Isaiah's direction in the earlier verses. Look at your friends, your family, your students, and your coworkers. Are some of them the "oppressed" who need encouragement? Are some of them the "fatherless" who are missing a loved one this Advent season? Or, better yet, is there some wrong you continue to do that needs to change? Is there a reason for you to hear the admonition to "learn to do right!"?

During this Christmas season, we look forward to celebrating the birth of Jesus—a great contrast to be sure. It is a time to recall how our all-powerful God came to earth as a helpless human, setting the stage for the contrast of life over death that he showed on Easter. It is a season of big contrasts: a king who comes in poverty, a Savior who arrives as a helpless child, a world of hatred and scorn being offered a taste of God's eternal peace. So don't adjust the contrast this season. Rejoice in God's love, and find a way to exhibit that joy and love in your own life and the lives of those around you.

> Oh, joy to know that you, my Friend,
> Are Lord, beginning without end,
> The first and last, eternal!
> And you at length—O gracious grace—

Will take me to that holy place,
The home of joys supernal.
Amen, Amen! Come and meet me,
Quickly greet me!
With deep yeaarning,
Lord, I look for your returning.
(Christian Worship 79:4)

Lift High the Cross

Lift high the cross; the love of Christ proclaim
Till all the world adore his sacred name.
George Kitchin, 1827–1912

About two months ago, it seemed like I couldn't drive anywhere without being inundated with signs that professed loyalty to a certain candidate. Whether it was at the national, state, or local level, people living in battleground states were the focus of an intense media blitz. Within days of the election being over, the signs disappeared. The fervor of the campaign was gone.

I fear that our day-to-day Christian lives are like this at times also. There are times when we seem energized by our faith. Perhaps some challenge rallies our innermost feelings to action. Perhaps a string of unusual blessings within the life of our congregation or church or school summons us to "lift high the cross." In our personal lives, the everyday ebb and flow may cause a particular energizing of a dormant desire to lift high the cross.

At Christmastime it's not unusual to hear someone say, "Don't forget the reason for the season" and "Keep Christ in Christmas." I see nothing wrong with the sentiment behind these sayings. Churches are crowded. Preachers spend a lot of time meticulously crafting their words to reach people whom they may not see

---

Text by George Kitchin, rev. Michael Newboldt. © 1974 Hope Publishing Co., Carol Stream, IL 60188. All rights reserved. Used by permission.

for another few months. Christians everywhere seem to do their best to show their support for their "candidate of choice." They lift high the cross.

Yet what about the days after Christmas? Will the "campaign signs" come down as quickly as they did from the November election?

Christ is not only the reason for the season but also the reason we live as redeemed children of God. To live our lives as if nothing happened is to ignore the whole point of that moment two thousand years ago. If we only lift high the cross during the high festivals of the year, then we fail to acknowledge the power of the Spirit in us and the love that came down that holy night.

God has called us to lift high the cross in his name, by his direction, and with his power, just as he called on his Son to carry the cross and suffer on it for our sakes.

The second part of the refrain in this powerful hymn says, "The love of Christ proclaim till all the world adore his sacred name." There are still a lot of people in our world who have no idea who Jesus is or what he has done for them. This Christmas is a time for lifting the cross to our students, our coworkers, our family, our neighbors, and our world full of people who need Jesus' light in their dark and hopeless lives.

Jesus is the reason you and I can live a life free of guilt, basking in the radiant glow of his forgiveness. So lift high the cross and proclaim his love, not only this Christmas but every Christmas and all throughout the year. Celebrate Christmas every day of your life by sharing Jesus with others.

Don't Sleep In!

And do this, understanding the present time. The hour has come for you to wake up from your slumber, because our salvation is nearer now than when we first believed. The night is nearly over; the day is almost here. So let us put aside the deeds of darkness and put on the armor of light.
Romans 13:11,12

With today being the last day of school before Christmas break, I'm guessing that a lot of teachers and students are looking forward to sleeping in tomorrow. The thing about sleeping in is that you always run the risk of missing something, whether it's a beautiful sunrise or a homemade breakfast.

Paul's words to the Romans remind us that there's a bit of urgency in our faith-lives. He just finished telling Christians to love one another and the people around them. Love is an action. We can't sleepwalk through a love for others that is vibrant. For a season that stresses peace, there's an urgency to the loving way we bring peace to one another.

I really like this passage at this time of the year. A lot of what we do at Christmas revolves around things we feel we must do. The number of people we have to see or buy presents for or send cards to can easily cause feelings of commitment rather than excitement. All the hustle of the season adds to an already busy schedule.

The gift of God's unfathomable love, made flesh in his Son, is the signal that the dark night is at an end. We are the bearers of that good news. God not only works *in* us to refresh us and renew us with that good news, he works *through* us as well. Through us, God's Spirit is alive. Through us, God is putting the finishing touches on his plan. How exciting, and humbling, to be in the thick of it all.

We each have favorite memories of Christmas from our youth. For me, those memories include popcorn balls on the way out of church, the gift I received of an exploding bridge to use with my army men, my first slot-car racing set, and the Christmas Eve programs at church. There was excitement and joy in knowing that Christmas was about to happen. If I had slept in, I would have missed all the excitement of Christmas.

This Christmas, wake up. The long night of suffering will be broken again when the dawn of Christmas breaks. Just as the radiance of the angels pierced the darkness of that night, so God's love pierces our souls. We're the real reason for the season. God's Son came to earth to live and die for us. Rejoice! You are in a place where God is at work. Rejoice in your calling as one of his children. Rejoice with those around you as you see what God is doing through them.

A New Year's Resolution

I want to know Christ and the power of his resurrection and the fellowship of sharing in his sufferings, becoming like him in his death, and so, somehow, to attain to the resurrection from the dead. Philippians 3:10,11

I have never been one for New Year's resolutions. Maybe it is the admission of past failures, but the idea of a short-term fix has never appealed to me.

As a sinner, however, I am constantly aware of my shortcomings and the many times I fall short of God's expectations for me. The renewing power that is mine through Baptism allows me to consider a resolution every day, not just on New Year's Day.

Paul's message to the Philippian Christians gives us insight into the kind of resolution that Paul thought was important. One: "Know Christ and the power of his resurrection." Part of this is knowledge. I need to immerse myself in the Word. I need to be faithful in worship and open my heart and mind to the words I hear and say in worship instead of just going through the motions. I need to give the Holy Spirit a chance to work in my heart. But there's more to it than just knowledge. I need to realize that the power of Christ's resurrection comes to me through repentance and forgiveness. Regular confession and attendance at the Holy Supper help me experience this. The power that I experienced in my baptism also stays with me today as a gift of the Holy Spirit. With this gift I am assured on a daily basis of the power of his resurrection.

Two: "Know . . . the fellowship of sharing in his sufferings." This comes to us through the sharing of faith that goes on when we spend time with other redeemed Christians. Sharing the power of Christ in our lives and God's pronouncement of his forgiveness with one another are things we need to do a lot more of. At the same time, sharing in this suffering also means being bold enough to admit my sin, to feel the depths of being lost to sin, and to see the effects of my sin in my own life. Christ suffered because of my sin. I need to face up to that and acknowledge my desperate need for forgiveness.

Three: "[To become] like him in his death, and so, somehow, to attain to the resurrection from the dead." Most of this resolution is out of my hands. At my baptism I became like Christ in his death, as I also became dead to sin. By grace I share in Christ's resurrection and look forward to my own life eternal. I need to live in the certain confidence that is mine through Baptism. I need to continue to tap into the Spirit's power rather than pretend I'm okay on my own. I need to seek God's direction rather than try to forge my own path.

At some time during this year I will question where God is leading me. At some point I will be disappointed in those around me. And sooner or later, I will be in conflict with coworkers, students, and family. At all of these times, I need to remember Paul's words and resolve to make this a *new* year in the same way that God's power of forgiveness has made my life a *new* life.

My New Year's resolution is really an everyday resolution. I resolve to make each day a new day with

Christ. Later the apostle Paul adds, "Forgetting what is behind and straining toward what is ahead, I press on toward the goal to win the prize for which God has called me heavenward in Christ Jesus" (verses 13,14). That's the kind of New Year's resolution I can get into.

General

Walk in Wisdom

He who walks with the wise grows wise, but a companion of fools suffers harm. *Proverbs 13:20*

For the foolishness of God is wiser than man's wisdom, and the weakness of God is stronger than man's strength. *1 Corinthians 1:25*

As I practice my own form of spiritual discipline by writing devotions, some weeks the titles just seem to come to mind as if God wanted them written specifically for that time of year or time of my life. This week's title is a good example of that. Discussing *wisdom* in a devotion during the season of the church year when we celebrate the wise men seems to be a perfect fit. Discussing wisdom at a time when we are nearing the end of a semester filled with many hours of study makes the text even more appropriate. We hope that our students surround themselves with other wise people and wise habits as they prepare for lifetimes of learning and serving.

And then there is the New Year's resolution I never made. If I was to set a resolution for myself, I guess *walk in wisdom* wouldn't be a bad place to start.

Consider your own life. Think of times when you haven't been really happy or weren't at the top of your game. Who were you walking with? Was it the wise or the foolish? God, in his great love for us, has provided us with wise people to walk with. His Spirit is alive in them and works through them to guide us along the way. It might be relatives, coworkers, students, or friends.

The problem is that we like to try hanging around with the fools once in awhile too. Imagine if those first wise men had listened to that fool Herod. Things may have gone a little differently.

So it is with us. When we choose to put ourselves in the company of foolishness (often of our own making), we run the risk of alienating ourselves from God. Instead of walking in his love, we put our faith in harm's way.

No matter how many times I remind myself that God knows what he is doing, I continue to rely on the wisdom and strength of the world. But at the end of the day, I crawl back to God, beaten by the ways of the world and discouraged in my attempts to make sense of life and its setbacks. I continue to fail to be the kind of person God wants me to be. Nevertheless, God's grace abounds. He forgives me and, through his Spirit, renews my spirit so that I am able to once again walk in his wisdom.

If you're struggling to walk in wisdom, find your strength in God's love. Turn to those godly people with whom God has surrounded you. Find someone who is living a life of wisdom and walk with him or her. Or find someone who is struggling and pray that God leads you to be a wise partner for that person.

There are plenty of fools to hook up with. Make this year a time when you become a wise person yourself. Walk with Jesus in the "foolishness" of the gospel; it's God's wisdom for us.

General

The Upside of Anger

*You were taught, with regard to your former way of life, to put off your old self, which is being corrupted by its deceitful desires; to be made new in the attitude of your minds; and to put on the new self, created to be like God in true righteousness and holiness. Therefore each of you must put off falsehood and speak truthfully to his neighbor, for we are all members of one body. "In your anger do not sin": Do not let the sun go down while you are still angry, and do not give the devil a foothold.
Ephesians 4:22-27*

I recently watched the 2005 movie titled *The Upside of Anger*. Without revealing too much of the film's plot, let me say that the main story is about a woman with four daughters whose husband suddenly leaves her. The movie recounts the three years immediately following that event and how her anger affects her and all those around her. Her bitterness changes her personality, causes her loneliness to be magnified, and strains every relationship she is in. The title of the movie comes from a school report that one of her daughters writes on anger.

While reflecting on the movie, I thought about how many times my anger at a situation or an individual has changed my personality. My inability to let it go has plagued me. To be honest, there are certain events in my life of which I still haven't let go. The anger I felt at being mistreated or hurt has, in some cases, not gone away. This failure to let go continues to color the way I interact with people.

There are other times I hide behind the term *righteous anger*. Those are times when I feel vindicated in my anger, times when I've justified my anger with some inborn principle that only I know. It's not that I don't believe in righteous anger; there are plenty of examples of it in the Bible. Rather, what I doubt is my own discernment; the line between sin-provoked anger and so-called righteous anger can easily become blurred.

Think about who or what is angering you right now. Is there resentment or anger seething in the backstory of your life? Is it a family member, student, coworker, or even a world event that has you all riled up? Maybe it is something beyond your control. Maybe an accident or illness has raised your ire. How is that affecting your relationships? What is it doing to your ministry? Did the sun go down on your anger last night? Will that same thing happen again tonight?

Paul says the goal should be to put away our anger. The only way to accomplish this is to replace our anger with something positive and good. We need to replace our anger with the love, forgiveness, and peace that are ours through the grace of God. Then we can go to sleep confident in the peace that is ours through Christ Jesus.

There is an upside of anger for Christians. We have the power, through God's Holy Spirit, to walk away from our anger, to keep it from driving our emotions and lifestyles. The upside of our anger is the peace that can fill the holes left behind when anger eats away at us. Ask the Lord to remove all the anger that you have stored up inside. Some of it may have been there for years. Some of the anger you harbor could give you a brand-new reason to be angry today. Either way, ask the Lord to fill the empty room in your heart with his love and his peace.

General

Set Free by the Truth

To the Jews who had believed him, Jesus said, "If you hold to my teaching, you are really my disciples. Then you will know the truth, and the truth will set you free." *John 8:31,32*

Have you ever had a "Tell-Tale Heart" experience? You know, one of those times when guilt was consuming you?

When I was around nine or ten years old, I was tossing "dirt bombs" across the street with my friend. In a moment of unbelievably bad timing, a car came down the street just as I launched a bomb. Of course, I ran and hid like any self-protecting kid would do. The car stopped and, driven by some pangs of conscience, I revealed myself as the culprit. There was no damage to the car, but the driver suggested I tell my parents and then drove off.

I had no intention of telling my parents, but as the day wore on, the guilt increased and I eventually confessed. The relief in confessing was matched by my parents' understanding and forgiveness. Though I was also duly punished.

I wonder if I would do the same thing now. As an adult, I seem to have developed a much better coping mechanism that knows how to neutralize a guilty conscience. Yet there are always lingering feelings of guilt in my life caused by sins, past and present. Some of the guilt is cleverly hidden in the recesses of my soul where I can ignore it. But as long as there is guilt, I am not free. I am still burdened and held captive by my own conscience. I know that Christ has the power to set me free. Why then is it that I don't always feel set free? Perhaps, like much of the rest of the world, I have confused feeling sorry with confessing.

The Greek word for repentance is *metanoia,* which means "a change of mind, genuine grief, a turning away from sin, the willingness to make restitution for wrongs committed." Far too many times in my life I've said the words "I'm sorry" with no intention of turning away from the very sin that caused the problem. They are easy words to say but harder words to be truly sincere about. Perhaps the guilt I feel comes more from my own realization that I don't want to make restitution, that I'm too stubborn to change, and that I'm not really sorry.

How about you? Is there a deep-rooted sense of guilt that you wrestle with? Is there a relationship that's been harmed? We talk about the consequences of sin. The biggest consequence may be the guilt many of us feel.

Now that you're feeling bad, plowing through your checkered past and dredging up old sins not yet accounted for, it's time to hear something more positive: Jesus is the Way, the Truth, and the Life. If we hold to Christ's teaching and become his disciples, those three words—*way, truth,* and *life*—offer great comfort to guilty consciences. Because of Jesus we don't have to be afraid to face up to the wrongs we've committed. Jesus is the *way* to escape from sin. The *truth* is that he loves us and died to remove our guilt—all of it. And through his grace, we can be sure that eternal *life* in heaven is ours. He sets us free. And no accusing conscience or finger-pointing devil can take that freedom away from us.

That's why we have the Epiphany season. It teaches us about Christ's living among us. It reminds us that his love is here among us in the full and free forgiveness he offers to us each and every day.

Teach Us Your Ways, O Lord

*"Come, let us go up to the mountain of the L*ORD*, to the house of the God of Jacob. He will teach us his ways, so that we may walk in his paths." Micah 4:2*

Do you ever feel like Sisyphus? He's the man in Greek mythology who angered the gods and was sentenced to an eternal punishment. The punishment involved pushing a large boulder up a hill. But each time the boulder reached the top, it would roll back down. Then poor Sisyphus would have to start the entire process over again.

Do you have a boulder to deal with in your life? Some of us have more than one—enough sadness, disappointment, and dissatisfaction to keep a person in perpetual frustration for a lifetime. All of this is because of the presence of sin. Yet we think we know how to handle these boulders—just get behind them and push them out of the way using human leverage, human resources, and human plans. But then the boulders come crashing down and we have to start all over again. When will we learn?

How about you? Are you tired of pushing the boulders and blazing your own path? God is there for us. We can walk his paths, but only if we let him teach us his ways.

Letting Christ teach me his ways depends on two people: I have to be a good student and he needs to be a good teacher. A good student needs to be patient. A good student needs to trust the teacher. A good student needs to study and do the homework. A good student realizes that the teacher has all the information needed to pass the test. A good student surrenders pride and ego. A good student asks questions and seeks help.

A good teacher doesn't just tell a student what to do; he or she models it in word and action. A good teacher puts a student into situations where that student can try out newfound knowledge. A good teacher knows that every student will struggle and even fail at times, so he or she offers support and forgiveness. A good teacher knows that every student is capable of getting off track, and so, gently brings his or her students back and forgives them. A good teacher provides the textbook and notes that will allow the student to succeed. A good teacher provides extra help and time when a student is faltering.

Christ is a good teacher—the best. He provides a spiritual learning path in his Word that Sisyphus would covet. We need to submit to Christ, read his book, apply his lessons to life, ask the hard questions, and listen for his wise counsel.

Are you pushing a boulder or two uphill right now? Head on up to the top of the Lord's mountain where Jesus does all the heavy lifting. His mountain dwarfs the boulders of your life. He provides strength and endurance to help you overcome your everyday struggles with all of those frustrating boulders. Stop and sit a while . . . at his feet. Learn what his ways and his paths are like.

Saint Titus and the January Doldrums

But God, who comforts the downcast, comforted us by the coming of Titus, and not only by his coming but also by the comfort you had given him. . . . By all this we are encouraged. In addition to our own encouragement, we were especially delighted to see how happy Titus was, because his spirit has been refreshed by all of you. I had boasted to him about you, and you have not embarrassed me. But just as everything we said to you was true, so our boasting about you to Titus has proved to be true as well. And his affection for you is all the greater when he remembers that you were all obedient, receiving him with fear and trembling. 2 Corinthians 7:6,7,13-15

A researcher recently determined that January 23 is the most depressing day of the year for people living in the northern hemisphere. Apparently the distance between holidays (between Christmas/New Year's and Valentine's Day) and the type of weather that afflicts us during late January make this an especially difficult time of year. For teachers and kids in school it may be even worse; there are no breaks in sight for a long time.

This week is also the week in the church year when we celebrate the work of Saint Timothy and Saint Titus and the conversion of Saint Paul. Saint Titus, in particular, is a good fit for January.

Titus was one of Paul's closest associates, and he was an early-church troubleshooter. Paul sent Titus to take care of problems in Corinth. He later established the church in Crete before spending time in what is present-day Yugoslavia. It appears Titus was a wise man and a skilled negotiator who was able to bring peace and joy wherever he went. No wonder Paul used his name is verse 6 when talking about comforting the downcast! Titus was a great example of someone whom we all should emulate.

Has God perhaps called you to be a Titus. As you look around, you may see family members, friends, students, or coworkers dealing with issues that cause them to be downcast. Maybe it is just the weather, but it could be more. Titus seems to have had the patience to persevere and the ability to use God's power to bring joy and peace to situations that desperately needed both. That may be why God has called you to the place and time you are in right now.

Being a Titus can be draining too. Maybe you tire of being the one who provides joy and peace for others. Just as you may tire, so did Titus. (And so did Paul; that's why God gave him Titus.) It's hard being positive all the time. Realize that Titus received his gifts from God. And without the gift of faith, those other special gifts would have been useless.

I don't know who chose January as the month in which we celebrate these saints. But it seems to me that in Titus' case, it is a very appropriate time of the year. Maybe you are looking back on January 23rd and saying it really wasn't that bad. Or maybe this devotion finds you in the depths of sadness. Either way, know that God's love and joy are there for all of us at all times. Sometimes we need a Titus to remind us of that. And sometimes we are the Tituses for others.

Winter

Press On Toward the Goal

Not that I have already obtained all this, or have already been made perfect, but I press on to take hold of that for which Christ Jesus took hold of me. Brothers, I do not consider myself yet to have taken hold of it. But one thing I do: Forgetting what is behind and straining toward what is ahead, I press on toward the goal to win the prize for which God has called me heavenward in Christ Jesus.
Philippians 3:12-14

    Last Saturday, during one of my forays outside into a 12-inch blizzard, I looked at the length of my 90-foot driveway and sighed. I had gotten enough of it shoveled for a car to get through but still had about half of it to go. I was already tired, frustrated with the weather, and not at all motivated to keep going. For whatever reason, the title for this devotion, "Press On Toward the Goal," resonated in my mind. As I was buffeted by wind and snow, I was resigned to the fact that I had little choice. It would have to get done sooner or later, so I might as well stay with it and finish it. But sometimes the snow was blowing so hard that it obscured that simple goal.
    I'm pretty sure my attitude of resignation was not really what Paul was talking about in this passage. Perhaps the difference is in the prize. A clean driveway in a blustery Wisconsin winter doesn't quite compare to eternity in heaven.
    Our lives carry many of the same pitfalls. If we don't sense a worthwhile prize, our attitude and enthusiasm for life easily wane. When our goals become obscured, we feel confused as to where life is

taking us. When reasonable goals become impossible to reach, we feel cheated. Life, like that snowstorm, can seem unrelenting in its desire to hinder our races toward the ultimate goal.

Paul certainly knew that. It is why he wrote these words to the Philippians. In a book that is known for its "joy" theme, Paul gives us insight for handling life and it's challenges. There are three important points that help us through life's blizzards. First, Paul acknowledges that he has a long way to go and that he's not perfect. He realizes that he's still going to make mistakes along the way. We're going to continue to be besieged by sin, temptation, and our human weakness. But we press on because Christ pressed on. He "took hold" of me. What a great phrase! Can't you just see Christ pulling you along through life's race? Hopefully, you can see this and feel this in your life.

Second, Paul tells us that he forgets what is behind. Dwelling on past sins and mistakes is not going to make them go away. Guilt has a way of paralyzing us. Whether that guilt is self-induced or given to us by someone else, it can bring us to the brink of despair. God, through his Son, has forgiven us. If we try and run the race with baggage, we're doomed from the start. Christ has removed all our sin and guilt. Experience that freedom by going to him with your confession and hearing him remind you that you're forgiven. It will give you that extra kick you need to finish the race.

Third, Paul reminds us to "press on." That's easier to do when you have a goal in sight. What's your goal? Is it just to get to Easter break with your sanity? Is it to get to the end of the school year or just to get through this athletic season? Is it retirement or a new job? How about getting over some sickness or a nagging injury? How about working out a damaged relationship? These, in themselves, are all worthy goals. But the goal Paul has in mind is essential to our lives in Christ and relationships to others. Paul's goal is for us to be united with Christ in everlasting love. That's why Christ "took hold" of us. He wants us to experience, with him, true love and everlasting life. His love for us is so great that it overshadows all else. That is why we press on. Whether at home, in the classroom, or in the world, we press on because he loved us enough to provide the prize at the end of the race.

People often use the metaphor of the race of life. Occasionally you might even hear about hurdles in that race. I'd rather use the steeplechase as an example. That's the race where you go down and up. You run through water and dry land. Competitors often fall during the race. That's life as I know it. I stumble and fall. I get real low sometimes when things don't work out and when there always seems to be another obstacle in my way. The race gets even harder if I look down. Then I forget where I'm going and what the ultimate goal is. Those are the times when Christ, through his Holy Spirit, takes hold of me and provides the strength for me to "press on toward the goal."

General

Am I the Weeds?

"A farmer went out to sow his seed. As he was scattering the seed, some fell along the path, and the birds came and ate it up. Some fell on rocky places, where it did not have much soil. It sprang up quickly, because the soil was shallow. But when the sun came up, the plants were scorched, and they withered because they had no root. Other seed fell among thorns, which grew up and choked the plants. Still other seed fell on good soil, where it produced a crop—a hundred, sixty or thirty times what was sown. He who has ears, let him hear. . . . The one who received the seed that fell among the thorns is the man who hears the word, but the worries of this life and the deceitfulness of wealth choke it, making it unfruitful." *Matthew 13:3-9,22*

    A few weeks ago as I sat down at church, I immediately noticed that the entire order of service was different—creed, confessions, sermon, Communion, readings, prayers. They were all there, just in different places. Then I remembered that it was the weekend our praise group was going to be leading the music—drums, guitar, piano, people clapping and singing—the whole nine yards. Well, I decided right then and there that I wasn't going to like the service. I settled into my this-isn't-the-way-it's-supposed-to-be-done mode and decided I wasn't going to get anything out of the service. While I understood the reason for changing the order of service, I kept thinking about all the historic reasons the liturgy is the way it is; I just couldn't get past them.
    My stubbornness continued, I'm ashamed to admit, until the song right before Communion. I really liked

the words of the song. The words spoke to me in a very personal way. The point is, it wasn't the order of the service or the musical style that kept me from growing in my faith that day, it was me. And that got me thinking about this parable about the farmer.

I never really thought this parable was about me. It was always about people who didn't have faith, people who through some unfortunate circumstance didn't bear the full message of God or had their small faith choked out. But it seems that I may be my own weeds. I may be letting Satan cause me to doubt the promises of God's Word by focusing on their delivery rather than their message. The disciples had the same problem. When they asked Jesus why he taught in parables, Jesus explained that not everyone understands on the same level or in the same way.

I believe we need to understand that regarding our students as well. God's love may be shown to us by the least likely student in the least likely way. God may also present us with opportunities to share his love at times when we may least expect them. The challenge is not to let our own insecurities and stubbornness become weeds that choke out the beautiful message of love and forgiveness that was planted in our lives at our baptisms. Be open to letting God's Word fall into your lives in different ways, in different places, by different people. Rejoice that God surrounds you with his love by using a variety of approaches and people.

General

Soaring in the Spirit

Do you not know? Have you not heard? The Lord is the everlasting God, the Creator of the ends of the earth. He will not grow tired or weary, and his understanding no one can fathom. He gives strength to the weary and increases the power of the weak. Even youths grow tired and weary, and young men stumble and fall; but those who hope in the Lord will renew their strength. They will soar on wings like eagles; they will run and not grow weary, they will walk and not be faint. *Isaiah 40:28-31*

Our house lies directly below one of the major approach lanes into the main Milwaukee airport. As a result, I have had the opportunity many times to look out an airplane window and see my house, my neighborhood, and its surrounding area as my plane is descending into the airport. From this sky view, everything looks tranquil and well tended. I can't tell whose grass needs to be cut, which roads are in need of repair, in which house people are fighting, or whose child might be lost. I also can't see that carpet in my house that needs to be replaced, my messy tool bench, or my treadmill that reminds me that I need to keep exercising. While I'm soaring above in that plane, I am allowed, if even just in my imagination, to escape the reality of the world below me.

By the grace of God, and through the love of his Son and the power of his Spirit, I can do the same kind of soaring in my life. I have times, and I'm betting you do too, when I'm overwhelmed by feelings of inadequacy, disappointment, shame, and grief. I see the habits in my life that need to be replaced, the messy relationships that need to be cleaned up, and the lack of regular spiritual exercise that needs to be remedied. My first solution is to try to rise above these problems on my own. Predictably, the result is a disaster, just as if I were trying to fly on my own. In my personal world of sin and its consequences, I am hopelessly grounded.

It happens so frequently that I must be similar to those Israelites to whom Isaiah was talking. It's almost as though he was incredulous in his own words: "Do you not know? Have you not heard?" I develop a tendency to forget that the only way to escape guilt and sin—the only way to fly—is to soar like an eagle by the power of the Spirit.

When I "soar," those are the moments of true joy in my life. I am uplifted by the phrase "given and shed for you for the forgiveness of your sins," by thoughts of my baptism and its blessings, and after I've confessed my sins and the pastor tells me and the other members of the congregation that our sins are washed away. Those moments when God says to me, "Have you not heard? I love you."

Surely we've all experienced the lows of being trapped, stumbling and falling through life as we try to navigate on our own. Well, guess what? It's time to soar, and this is not merely an exercise in your imagination. It is made real for us in Christ's own body and blood. It is made real for us in Jesus' surrogate life, sacrificial death, and victorious resurrection from the dead. We are truly uplifted when we are allowed to experience a taste of what our eternal lives will be—an everlasting flight, soaring with the Spirit.

General

Reenrollment Night—Not for Everyone

Christ died for sins once for all, the righteous for the unrighteous, to bring you to God. He was put to death in the body but made alive by the Spirit. 1 Peter 3:18

It's that time of the year when schools start gearing up for the next school year. Nevermind that the first semester is barely over; it's time to get people thinking about next year. It's time to fill out the enrollment form again, pay the deposit, and prove that, once again, you want to be a student. From preschool to graduate school, you must demonstrate once again that you really want to return next year.

We tend to get caught up in finding ways to make people reassure us. Some of it is out of necessity; school administrators need to have an idea of what enrollment will be next year. Personal relationships can get all tangled up, so we make people convince us over and over of their love, or their trustworthiness, or their ability. Sometimes teachers give assignment after assignment or test after test just to prove that their students have mastered the curriculum. Sometimes parents expect their children to jump the same hurdles time and time again before they fully trust them. In our personal relationships, it's often much easier to distrust than to trust. And if someone has let us down just once, it's even harder to win our trust back.

Yet, as Christians, we're never expected to reenroll. If God would ask us to prove, even once, that we deserve to be his children, we'd be in trouble.

Fill out an application for enrollment in God's family? Our occupation would be *sinner* . . . and that's the end of that!

About the only thing we could do is apply for financial aid, admitting our total unworthiness and turning to God for help. God's love for us takes care of everything, including our full tuition fee, which reserves for us a permanent place in his family. Our onetime enrollments happened at our baptisms, when you and I became part of this very special family. We never have to reenroll. We don't have to sit around nervously waiting for an acceptance letter.

Remember, God has done the very same for all those children in your class, all the loved ones in your life, and all those people that sit by you in church each week. It's a onetime thing; and it's all been completed for us. He died for a whole world of sinners, making enrollment into God's kingdom of life and peace a real open-door policy.

General

Shine Like Stars

> Therefore, my dear friends, as you have always obeyed—not only in my presence, but now much more in my absence—continue to work out your salvation with fear and trembling, for it is God who works in you to will and to act according to his good purpose. Do everything without complaining or arguing, so that you may become blameless and pure, children of God without fault in a crooked and depraved generation, in which you shine like stars in the universe as you hold out the word of life—in order that I may boast on the day of Christ that I did not run or labor for nothing. *Philippians 2:12-16*

What parent or teacher hasn't experienced the child or student who is an "Eddie Haskell" type? You know, the kind of kid who is perfect when you're in the room and is conniving when you're gone. Paul compliments the Philippians for their obedience in both situations—in his presence and in his absence. Yet he reminds them, and us, that we need to keep working at our spiritual maturity. What a great message for those who are moving on to some new phase of their lives! We, and they, cannot take spiritual growth for granted; we, and they, must always find opportunities to grow. At times this may be difficult, or even scary, but work we must.

For those who are soon going to be taking another step toward independence and a more productive role in the bigger world, leaving their schools or their homes is not the end of their spiritual journeys. In many ways, learning is another beginning as they venture into situations where they will not be quite so insulated by school and home. They must, as Paul says, "will and . . . act." It is not enough to simply know what to do; the time is coming soon when they will have to put what they've learned from us into action.

These verses remind all of us that it is easy to be frustrated with God's plans for our lives. It's much easier to complain instead of humbly acknowledging God's will. When our children eventually leave us, they are often convinced they know it all and are ready to take on the world. Yet the world they are entering often pollutes their image of God and undermines their hopes in his plan. The result of this dissatisfaction with God is that their spiritual growth will be stunted, and they will begin to focus on things that have nothing to do with God or his plan.

Paul exhorts us to be "children of God." Not perfect children but children who have a dedicated devotion to carrying out God's will. Isn't this why we are Christian teachers and parents? We hope, through the guidance of the Spirit, that the people of the next generation will strive to be children of God who acknowledge God's role in their lives and seek to do his will.

Finally, we get to the words of our title, to "shine like stars." As our students find themselves in the middle of a world that can only disappoint and confuse them, they need to draw on the lessons we have taught them—actually, they're really God's lessons, drawn from his Holy Word. With those well-taught lessons in tow, they will have the energy to shine like stars, brilliantly, from him who is the source of light.

While I've been connecting this passage to our children and students, I haven't forgotten about the roles in which we serve as teachers and parents. Paul's words penetrate our souls as well. We too need to continue to work at our salvation. Our spiritual growth is not finished. Before we can ask our children to shine like stars, we must do some shining of our own.

At this time of the school year, it is easier to be dull and listless rather than shiny, bright stars in the heavens. We forget too easily that we are not the power source that lights us up. Our brilliance in the night sky comes from God—from the joy of knowing that we have a Savior named Jesus, from the promise of eternal life, and from the peace and hope we treasure even while we remain on this earth. God and his Spirit provide all the energy we ever need to shine like the stars. With that kind of candlepower, you and I will be bright enough for our students to see us sparkling brilliantly as we hold out the Word of Life before them.

'Tis Good, Lord, to Be Here

After six days Jesus took with him Peter, James and John the brother of James, and led them up a high mountain by themselves. There he was transfigured before them. His face shone like the sun, and his clothes became as white as the light. Just then there appeared before them Moses and Elijah, talking with Jesus. Peter said to Jesus, "Lord, it is good for us to be here. If you wish, I will put up three shelters—one for you, one for Moses and one for Elijah." While he was still speaking, a bright cloud enveloped them, and a voice from the cloud said, "This is my Son, whom I love; with him I am well pleased. Listen to him!" When the disciples heard this, they fell facedown to the ground, terrified. But Jesus came and touched them. "Get up," he said. "Don't be afraid." When they looked up, they saw no one except Jesus. Matthew 17:1-8

It's been a dreary kind of February here lately. From the two straight weeks of very below-normal temperatures, to the every-other-day snow showers, to the school closings because of subzero temperatures, people are getting tired of winter. I'm tired of all the dirty cars, the lack of sunshine and warmth. Oh, well, that's winter in the Midwest!

Sunday is the day in the church year when we celebrate the transfiguration of Christ. On the surface it doesn't seem like a particularly important story. Yet in this reading we hear God's voice and see Christ flanked on either side by two great Old Testament prophets.

So what do these two occurrences—the transfiguration and winter in the upper Midwest—have in common? And if there is any commonality to them, what do these seemingly unrelated events have to say to us?

I heard the words of Peter, "Lord, it is good for us to be here," and asked myself if I could honestly say those same words while staring out my window. When the weather isn't what we want or the circumstances in our jobs aren't as we would like them to be, it's easy to get wrapped up in negative thoughts. But Peter was on the other side of things. He was so excited about "being there" that he wanted to make it permanent. Peter must have been thinking, "How can it get any better than this?"

There are times we may feel like that too. Maybe we're on the perfect vacation, or have the perfect house, or the perfect class of kids, or the perfect day, or the perfect . . . (You fill in the blank in your own way.). We would prefer to have those special times last forever.

Notice, however, that almost before Peter finishes his sentence, God breaks the mood by telling the disciples, "This is my Son. . . . Listen to him!" In that instant, Peter's idea about building a memorial evaporated. The understanding that they were in God's presence was more important than the place where they were standing. Listening to God's Son was far more important than the idyllic setting could ever be.

There's nothing wrong with liking one type of weather more than another, but when our surroundings cause us to lose sight of our callings, then we've got a problem. When the weather or the people we work with or the makeup of our class causes us not to hear the voice of God, not to listen to his Son, then we're a lot like Peter.

God does speak to us—every day—through his Word and sacraments. He reaches out to us and asks us to listen. That's really what makes any place and any relationship come alive. The presence of God in that place or in that relationship allows us to look past what we don't like and to see and hear things from the perspective of a redeemed child of God.

God came to Elijah in a still small voice. He does the same with us. If we're too busy thinking about our surroundings, we could miss the message. Listen to God's Son and appreciate the calling he has given you. Whether it's snowy and 10 degrees below zero or sunny and 80 degrees, his Word of promise and truth transcends all times and all places.

Ash Wednesday

Looking Forward

Then Abraham spoke up again: "Now that I have been so bold as to speak to the Lord, though I am nothing but dust and ashes." *Genesis 18:27*

The LORD God formed the man from the dust of the ground and breathed into his nostrils the breath of life, and the man became a living being. *Genesis 2:7*

Being involved in education as a student, teacher, or administrator for virtually all of my life, Ash Wednesday didn't always have a deep, theological meaning for me. Instead, it signaled the beginning of the end of that interminably long period between Christmas and Easter. It meant that the end was in sight and that spring break was not too far off. The significance of Ash Wednesday was often obscured by the notion that I was about to escape the stranglehold of winter.

Of course, with age we like to think that occasional bursts of wisdom come to us. So maybe Ash Wednesday isn't just a gateway to spring break but a gateway to understanding who I am.

Abraham acknowledged his worthlessness to God: "I am nothing but dust and ashes." That's the main message of Ash Wednesday: I am no more than the dirt, dust, and salt that I sweep out of my garage after a long winter. The wind scatters those particles all over my yard, and I don't give that dirt another thought. That's really what I am as a sinful human—someone not really worth another thought. Yet, like Abraham, I have the audacity to try to talk to God.

Imagine some of that dirt in my garage asking me to give it some of my attention. I would sweep it into oblivion regardless of its plea; it means nothing to me.

Yet imagine if I could take all of that dirt I've ever swept away and mold it into something wonderful, then it might be worth trying to save. When God created man, he did it from something worthless, the dust of the ground. Think of that! You and I are rooted in something absolutely worthless—dust! Yet because of God's power, wisdom, and love, he made us something special. Even more amazing, he does it over and over again. Each time I show my true self—when I sin and return to a life of dirt, ashes, and dust—God swoops in and breathes the love of his forgiveness into me, making me—like Adam—a living being . . . again.

Now, take it one step further. Look at the members of your family, the people in your neighborhood, the students in your classroom, your coworkers. What do you see when you look at them? Do you see dirt, or do you see living beings?

If I'm honest with myself, I know that because of my own sinful heart, I sometimes treat these people like dirt. I need to look at other people with the eyes of one who himself was once dirt but who has now had new life breathed into him at baptism. I need to see those around me as cleansed through that same promise of God's forgiveness.

In some ways Ash Wednesday is the harbinger of spring. It's a time when I need to refocus on the dirty, dusty, and ashen me. But I can do that with an eye on the future, an eye on that Sunday morning when I will feel a new breath of gospel air from God that will announce my forgiveness and give me new life in him.

General

Building Our Faith and Our Future

"I know the plans I have for you," declares the Lord, "plans to prosper you and not to harm you, plans to give you hope and a future." Jeremiah 29:11

A few weeks ago I got some really disappointing news regarding some hopes and plans I had for the future. To be honest, I'm still struggling with the disappointment. But I'm also wondering when God will decide to reveal his plans to me.

Maybe it's just my human nature, but as much as I believe the words of this passage from Jeremiah's pen, I still feel like God is sometimes toying with me as I try to make sense of my life. Sometimes I just want to say to God, "Tell me. Tell me, NOW! What are these great plans you have for me?" Then I lie in bed at night, feeling helpless about my hopelessness and letting my disappointment obscure all the great things God has done in my life.

Well, enough of my pity party! Some of you have probably been surrounded by disappointment once or twice yourself. Or perhaps your life is not as fulfilling as you'd like. Or maybe everything is fine for you in your life and you can't relate to any of this! No matter where we are in life, these words still speak to us. They talk to us about faith—faith enough in God that we can have inner peace regardless of the situations we find ourselves in.

When we struggle, it is not because God is making it tough, it's because you and I are making it tough. The fact that we have a relationship with him at all is not because we love him; it is always because he loves us. My desire to have more control of my life flies in the face of letting God be in control of my life. But just saying all these things and believing them on some level does not make them so. It is only when I, through the power of the Spirit, fight off my sinful human urge to control my life that I can find any peace at all.

I don't see myself as a very passive or accepting person. I tend to challenge and question almost everything. I think that reflects the fact that I'm pretty sure I always know best. I know a lot of parents and teachers like that. We assume that being authority figures makes us authorities on just about every topic. So when things don't go our ways, we go looking for someone to blame. We may even choose to blame God. That's a sign of a faith that needs to be reenergized.

God really does have plans for you and me. That's good news because God is a good God. The best part of those plans is that he loves us, forgives us, and plans to have us spend eternity with him. Our everyday existences will continue to have disappointments and frustrations. But life in him means that we can be renewed and reenergized in our faith. Life in him offers a glimpse of his plans for our futures, which include forgiveness and unconditional love.

"Smile, God loves you!" always seemed to be a shallow statement to me. Somehow I thought my faith relationship was deeper than that faddish statement. But that's really what Jeremiah is saying. When life sends us disappointment, we need to remember that God does have great futures planned for us. Even in the wake of great disappointment, you and I will be able to smile one of those knowing smiles that reflects the faith of someone who knows the future—a future that is in God's hands!

Know Christ, or Know What Christ Wants?

> But whatever was to my profit I now consider loss for the sake of Christ. What is more, I consider everything a loss compared to the surpassing greatness of knowing Christ Jesus my Lord, for whose sake I have lost all things. I consider them rubbish, that I may gain Christ and be found in him, not having a righteousness of my own that comes from the law, but that which is through faith in Christ—the righteousness that comes from God and is by faith. I want to know Christ and the power of his resurrection and the fellowship of sharing in his sufferings, becoming like him in his death, and so, somehow, to attain to the resurrection from the dead. *Philippians 3:7-11*

It's that time of the year when I spend a lot of time speaking with students about their future plans. I talk to a lot of seniors about their final college choices and talk with juniors about picking classes for next year. I always ask what their plans are for life after high school. We also start to meet with eighth graders and their parents to talk about the classes they'll take as freshmen next fall. It's a lot of talk about planning, dreaming, and the future. It's interesting to see the progression from the wide-eyed "I can do anything" attitude of eighth graders to the more reserved, calculated, and tempered plans of seniors. I try to get seniors to consider God's plan for their lives. I feel that many of the seniors and their parents spend a lot of time praying about their future. They reflect what many of us go through when faced with a tough decision in life; we try to discern the will of God. In fact, I hear a lot of people who try to make sense of what God wants them to do. They say it in just that way.

It's an easy trap to fall into. We can spend so much time worrying and fretting about figuring out what God wants us to do that we lose sight of what we're really supposed to be trying to learn. Judging by his words in Philippians, I don't think Paul spent a lot of time trying to figure out what God wanted him to do. As usual, Paul had it right. Trying to grasp God's undeserved love for him was a much better way to spend his time. "Knowing Christ" was even better than trying to know what God wanted him to do.

Don't get me wrong. There's nothing wrong with praying and asking for God's guidance in making decisions. The guidance of his Holy Spirit is the best direction we can have. But perhaps, just perhaps, spending a little more time in his Word and sacraments and in worship and fellowship would help us know Christ a little better. When, through the power of God's Holy Spirit, we know Christ better, the constant distraction of sin and worry dissipates. When our lives are lived with the goal of knowing and experiencing the power of his resurrection, knowing what God wants us to do with the days we have left is a little easier. The Spirit-filled life is driven by the reality of what Christ has done, not by trying to figure out what he would want us to do.

Paul's words are also an excellent description of Lent. During these 40 days we seek to share in his sufferings. When Easter comes, we will once again experience the power of God's inestimable love in Christ's resurrection and his victory over death. During this season of the church year, the weight of our sins is lifted from our backs and we realize all over again that what God really wants is for us to be his children—forgiven, loved, and cared for.

Lent

Set Your Mind on Things Above

Since, then, you have been raised with Christ, set your hearts on things above, where Christ is seated at the right hand of God. Set your minds on things above, not on earthly things. *Colossians 3:1,2*

    A couple of times a week I'm in our school weight room to supervise our athletes as they do conditioning and weight lifting. On several of the lifts, I remind the lifters to keep their heads and eyes up. By looking up, it allows them to keep their backs in better position. This, in turn, allows them to have better form, which translates into less chance for injury, better conditioning, and more weight being lifted. But it's a constant battle because the natural inclination is to let the weight pull you down. A lifter has to overcome the body's tendency to do it the wrong way. That's why we make sure each lifter has a spotter who reminds the lifter to do it correctly.

    During this Lenten season, we remember Christ and his passion journey to the cross. The weight of our sins and the knowledge of what lay before him must have been a heavy burden. He needed to focus on what was above—his heavenly Father. Christ's only chance for completing his challenge and making it to the goal was to keep his mind on things above.

    It's really not that different for you and me. While the challenge before us is not nearly the challenge that lay before Christ, the challenges we face daily can be substantial. We must keep our minds on things above. Rather than letting the weight of our sinful lives make us give in to the temptation to do things our way, we need to focus on keeping our eyes on Jesus. He has provided his Word and sacraments as our spotters; he has also given us his Holy Spirit to give us the inward desire we need to push through the burden of weight that the sinful world puts on our shoulders.

And what about our roles as spotters? Is there someone you know who needs to be "spotted" as he or she struggles with the burdens of life? Is it a spouse, child, coworker, or student? I'm not talking about someone who is just "down" about something. Rather, think of someone who may be struggling in his or her faith. Perhaps this person has forgotten to keep his or her mind on things above.

But to be effective servants, we need to do our spiritual exercises frequently and correctly so that we can help others with their burdens. Our spiritual exercises prepare us to be better spotters. Our calling is to help others and to point sinners to Jesus' cross. This Lenten season, keep your hearts and your minds on things above.

Lent

March Madness

Jesus said, "Now is the Son of Man glorified and God is glorified in him. If God is glorified in him, God will glorify the Son in himself, and will glorify him at once. My children, I will be with you only a little longer. You will look for me, and just as I told the Jews, so I tell you now: Where I am going, you cannot come. A new command I give you: Love one another. As I have loved you, so you must love one another." *John 13:31-34*

During this time of the year, followers of college and high school basketball get caught up in tournament fever. It is often called March Madness or the Road to the Final Four. It is a time of the year when sound bites and motivational sayings are everywhere. It is exciting because every game could be a team's last. There is a sense of unpredictability that magnifies every shot, every game, and every coaching move.

Most years March Madness goes on while Christians remember a different journey, a journey that involved one man on a solitary road that found its climax not at a trophy ceremony but on a cross on a hill. Lent is a time when we are reminded of the journey that Christ took. Much is made of the Final Four in basketball. Cheering throngs of devoted fans seek to propel their teams to victory. Undoubtedly, the scene for Christ on Palm Sunday was similar. Yet in less than a week, things took a much different turn, with a much more far-reaching conclusion than some simple basketball game's score.

It is our goal to put ourselves with Jesus on that path to his death and subsequent victory over Satan. Yet it is different for us. We know the outcome; we know he (and, by our baptisms, we) won. For the disciples, like the modern basketball fan, part of the excitement and trepidation with the journey was that the conclusion was unknown. Even if they believed Christ would rise, the disciples didn't really *know* that he would. Despite our believing and wanting our team to win, we don't really know what will happen. We may find it relatively easy to travel this journey during Lent, because we know Christ wins in the end. But we're listening only to our sinful selves if we think the journey is easy. Christ knew we couldn't follow him. We couldn't recreate his journey to Calvary. That is why he gave us the command to do the next best thing: "Love one another." That is Christ's message to us as we try to follow in his footsteps. He took the journey for us so that we would be able to love one another.

As you share the Lenten experience during this time of March Madness, remember that because we know the victory is ours, we can follow Christ's command to "love one another." No matter which Lenten series your church uses, the message is the same: "Where I am going, you cannot come." As mere human sinners, the journey would be impossible for us. It is our failure to follow the road laid out for us that caused his death in the first place. But Christ's love is so great that he paved the way to everlasting life for us. Lent is a time for introspection, to see how we have stumbled and fallen short of God's expectations for us. But thanks be to God that we can look to Jesus' cross and know that the victory is ours!

A simple phrase like "love one another" carries a whole new meaning when put into the context of Lent. As you ponder the inexplicable compassion that is God's love, reach out to your family, your friends, your students with words and actions of love that reflect Christ's journey for us. He took the final road for us so that we can love one another.

General

The Lord Is My Shepherd

The LORD is my shepherd, I shall not be in want. He makes me lie down in green pastures, he leads me beside quiet waters, he restores my soul. He guides me in paths of righteousness for his name's sake. Even though I walk through the valley of the shadow of death, I will fear no evil, for you are with me; your rod and your staff, they comfort me. You prepare a table before me in the presence of my enemies. You anoint my head with oil; my cup overflows. Surely goodness and love will follow me all the days of my life, and I will dwell in the house of the LORD forever. *Psalm 23*

What can I possibly say about this passage that hasn't been said before? This chapter is ingrained in so many Christians' minds and souls! It has been repeated so often that it may very well be that we take it for granted.

I wonder what mood David was in as he wrote this? I would speculate that it was one of two. Maybe he was so filled with joy about his life and relationship with God that the words just flowed out in pure adoration. Or perhaps he had been moping and complaining about all the miserable things in his life when he decided to start listing all the wonderful things God meant to him.

I find myself in that second mood quite often. I take for granted the many things God does for me. Instead, I dwell on all the things I'd like to see changed. David's words for me, "I shall not be in want," really should be more than words. Each week as I write one of these devotions I ask myself whether I'm just writing words or if I really believe them. I must admit, many times my answer is that I'm just writing words. My faith wavers as I deal with the uncertainties of life. Again, however, using David's words, "[God] restores my soul." Through his Word and sacraments and through opportunities to worship and fellowship with the other members of his body, he does just that—my soul is restored.

When I worry about taxes and college tuition and bills, I am in need of being reminded that "my cup" already "overflows." When I feel stressed out, I know that "he leads me beside quiet waters." When I worry about former students who are dealing with cancer or living in broken homes, when I worry about current students who are dealing with health problems or grades, when I worry about coworkers and their struggles with health and emotional issues, when I worry about loved ones and their struggles with relationships or hard decisions, I know that "goodness and love will follow me all the days of my life."

It occurs to me that there may be one other reason why David may have written this psalm. It is an acknowledged fact that the shepherd metaphor was often used in Old Testament times for the King. Perhaps David, burdened by the stresses of everyday "king stuff," needed to let go. Perhaps he needed to remind himself that there is a greater King. Perhaps these words helped remind David that he didn't have to do everything himself.

How about you? Are you trying to be in control of everything? Sit down, and read these words of David one more time. Put them into the context of your life.

General

Dad, Teacher, Saint?

This is how the birth of Jesus Christ came about: His mother Mary was pledged to be married to Joseph, but before they came together, she was found to be with child through the Holy Spirit. Because Joseph her husband was a righteous man and did not want to expose her to public disgrace, he had in mind to divorce her quietly. But after he had considered this, an angel of the Lord appeared to him in a dream and said, "Joseph son of David, do not be afraid to take Mary home as your wife, because what is conceived in her is from the Holy Spirit. She will give birth to a son, and you are to give him the name Jesus, because he will save his people from their sins." All this took place to fulfill what the Lord had said through the prophet: "The virgin will be with child and will give birth to a son, and they will call him Immanuel"—which means, "God with us." When Joseph woke up, he did what the angel of the Lord had commanded him and took Mary home as his wife. But he had no union with her until she gave birth to a son. And he gave him the name Jesus. *Matthew 1:18-25*

While many classrooms will be decorated in green this week, maybe even having traditional St. Patrick's Day parties, I'd like to center in on a different saint whose day is honored by all Christian denominations on March 19. The saint is Joseph, father of Christ.

As a father of two boys, I guess I've always been intrigued by Joseph. It must have been interesting to see Joseph teaching Jesus how to use carpentry tools, how to fish, how to worship, how to figure out what present to get his mother for her birthday, how to kick a ball, how to grill out . . . all those father-and-son things. I don't think it's hard for anyone who's a parent to imagine Jesus peppering Joseph with questions that started out, "Dad, how does a . . . ?"

What do we know about Joseph that helps us see why God chose him to be Jesus' surrogate father? Joseph was a plain, working man (a carpenter), yet he was of King David's royal lineage. He was a compassionate, caring man in the way he dealt with Mary when he found out she was pregnant. He was an obedient man of faith. Without question, he followed God's commands—even in moving his wife and son to Egypt. He loved Jesus as his own and raised him according to the Jewish laws and customs.

It seems like Joseph is a model for us in the classroom. As teachers, we are simple, working people. Yet, because of our baptisms, we are members of God's royal family. We are to be compassionate and caring in dealing with our students and their families. God has called us to be obedient to him—even to death! Every day we have opportunities to show that obedience in our classrooms through our words and actions. We are also given an opportunity to love our students as our own children and share with them the tenets of our faith. I believe that Joseph's example as a father gives us plenty of wonderful approaches to teaching.

Dad, teacher, saint? Joseph was all three. Pray that God leads you to follow Joseph's outstanding example in your classroom this week.

General

Be Strong and Courageous

"Be strong and courageous, because you will lead these people to inherit the land I swore to their forefathers to give them. Be strong and very courageous. Be careful to obey all the law my servant Moses gave you; do not turn from it to the right or to the left, that you may be successful wherever you go. Do not let this Book of the Law depart from your mouth; meditate on it day and night, so that you may be careful to do everything written in it. Then you will be prosperous and successful. Have I not commanded you? Be strong and courageous. Do not be terrified; do not be discouraged, for the LORD your God will be with you wherever you go." Joshua 1:6-9

For about 15 years now, ever since my last knee surgery, I have lifted weights two or three times a week. During that time I've seldom taken a break of more than three weeks. I started to do it as part of my therapy. Later I did it because I like the routine. Now I do it because it is supposed to be good for my bones and muscles as I get older. Whatever the reason, I had to work at it for my strength to increase.

God's message to Joshua was similar. In fact, God was so insistent about this imperative command that it was mentioned three times in this span of four verses. As his servants in an educational setting—as parents, as leaders at school or within our congregation—we are called on to be strong and courageous for the same reason that Joshua was: We are called to lead. By virtue of our calls into God's public ministry, our highest priority is to lead. We have been asked to lead people

121

to the promised land of God's love and forgiveness. So how do we become strong enough to do that?

God's Word gives us clear direction: "Obey all the law" and "meditate on it." That's our weight-lifting regimen. Get into the Word, regularly, and challenge yourself to do more lifting. Physical weight lifting only makes you stronger if you increase the weight or the repetitions. The same is true for your spiritual strength development. God promises that our spiritual weight lifting will lead us to being "prosperous and successful."

Some people find that having a personal trainer helps them do a better job of working out. God provides that as well. His Holy Spirit is with us to help us develop our strength to the point where we can be leaders. Having said that, I still find the final words to be the most comforting of this passage: *"Do not be terrified; do not be discouraged, for the L*ORD *your God will be with you wherever you go."* They sound so similar to Paul's words in Romans 8:35: *"Who shall separate us from the love of Christ? Shall trouble or hardship or persecution or famine or nakedness or danger or sword?"* And Christ Jesus himself tells us in Matthew 28:20, *"Surely I am with you always, to the very end of the age."*

All of this tells me that with the strength and courage that are mine through Christ, I can handle life. The fear that crops up because of sickness, family problems, financial burdens, uncertainty, or growing older is nothing new. When we worry, we are behaving just like the Israelites did in Joshua's time. We are afraid because we're not strong enough on our own.

This is the perfect time to remember that. As we look toward remembering Christ's passion in this Holy Week and then celebrating his triumph on Easter, we are embracing a time when we can understand how the weakness of the world, made manifest in Christ's death, makes us stronger through his love for us.

Be strong and courageous. Cherish your call from God to be a leader, and with his strength, be the best leader that you can be. But do it knowing that his strength is something you have to use as you work your way through life.

General

What's Your Name?

But now, this is what the Lord *says—he who created you, O Jacob, he who formed you, O Israel: "Fear not, for I have redeemed you; I have summoned you by name; you are mine. When you pass through the waters, I will be with you; and when you pass through the rivers, they will not sweep over you. When you walk through the fire, you will not be burned; the flames will not set you ablaze."* Isaiah 43:1,2

When I first started teaching, I was only nine years removed from my own graduation from the same school. A lot of my former teachers were still on the staff. One of the hardest things for me was calling those teachers by their first names. I grew up believing you call people mister, miss, or missus until they tell you otherwise. Even today I bristle when I hear teachers allow students to call them by nicknames rather than address them with formal titles such as *coach*. I guess I'm just more old-fashioned than I'd like to think.

We all have names. Many of us have nicknames. They are a part of who we are. Oftentimes our names reflect some family tradition or special people in our parents' lives. Nevertheless, God knows us all. He tells us that he calls us by name. He knows each of us personally and cares about each of us personally.

Recently, while attending an administrators' conference, I was impressed when during Communion, both the person distributing the bread and the pastor giving the wine addressed everyone by his or her first name. There were about three hundred people there, most of whom I didn't know. It seemed like quite a feat, until

I realized that we all had nametags hanging around our necks. Still, I appreciated the fact that they took the time to call me by name.

As teachers, we are working every day with young people whom God calls by name. He knows, cares for, and loves each one of them dearly—just as he does you and me. Do we always reflect that when we deal with those young people? Do we call our students by name with voices that communicate care for others of God's children? It is easy to assign names that are less than flattering for people who irritate us. Yet even when God gets irritated with us, he calls us by name in a loving, forgiving tone.

God called us by name when he made us his own through Baptism. He also called us by name when he chose us to be his ministers. There is something very comforting about knowing that God knows my name and uses it. It tells me that when I call God by name, he listens. It tells me that I am truly his child—someone whom he knows intimately because he died for me, someone he loves very dearly.

God has called us by name to this place, at this time, to do his work. Ask him to fill you with the power of his Holy Spirit so that you will bring glory and honor to his name as you daily go about doing his work.

General

Why Are You Here?

"I know the plans I have for you," declares the L ORD *, "plans to prosper you and not to harm you, plans to give you hope and a future."* Jeremiah 29:11

"Why are you here?" These were the beginning words of a litany during our Wednesday evening Lenten service this week. The thought kind of caught me off guard. It was a good question—one worth asking, not only at church but in our homes, classrooms, and pretty much wherever we are.

There are days I struggle with why I am where I am. I'm sure there are days the students at our school wonder why they're here as well. I know there are days our faculty and staff members wonder why they're here. There are people who wonder why they continue in what may often seem like dead-end relationships, or insignificant jobs, or even useless lives. We tend to dwell on those questions when we forget why Jesus was there, at the cross, and then victoriously outside the tomb. When we refocus on our Savior and why he chose to be where he was, it should give us the ability to see past the question of why we're here. Perhaps a better approach to the question would be to ask Jesus what he can do with us while we're here.

We tend to use the words of this text in Jeremiah for some reassurance regarding our future. It is frequently used at graduations or as a theme for a school year. It is generally used when we don't have a good answer to *Why are we here?* or at a time when the future is unknown. I think that simplifies this passage too much. How about taking a look at this passage with the understanding that God's real plan for me involves sending his Son to save me and his Spirit to guide me? That gives me the hope for a future that is a lot more important than merely knowing what God's plan for my life will be over the next 5, 10, or 15 years. That plan—the one that has my salvation firmly determined for the rest of eternity—is really the only plan that matters. In that plan I know that God will not abandon me. The proof is to be found in Jesus' love and in the sacrifice he made for you and me. That's the real strength of this wonderful passage. It may not answer the question *Why am I here?* But it does answer the question *Where will I be?*

Some of us may struggle our entire lives with trying to find the answer to the *Why am I here?* question. In faith we trust that God knows what he is doing and has a reason for putting us here, even though he may not tell us what it is.

During his journey to the cross, Jesus' disciples probably wondered for him, "Why are you here?" But not knowing the answer didn't change the outcome. Jesus was there for a very simple reason: because he loves each of us personally and with such passion that it drove him to his own execution. He knew exactly why he was there; it was to give us life, hope, and peace where we had no right to expect anything from him. It's a perfect plan—one that gives us every reason to have hope in a future that puts us in God's heavenly home with our own personal Savior for the rest of eternity.

The Majesty of Holy Week

> Then one of the seraphs flew to me with a live coal in his hand, which he had taken with tongs from the altar. With it he touched my mouth and said, "See, this has touched your lips; your guilt is taken away and your sin atoned for." Then I heard the voice of the Lord saying, "Whom shall I send? And who will go for us?" And I said, "Here am I. Send me!" *Isaiah 6:6-8*

Guilt can be a powerful thing. People often use it as a motivator. I've used guilt to get students, or teachers, to do things for me. Or perhaps I have thought their guilt would benefit them in the long run.

But there's a big difference between being guilty and being motivated by guilt. Martin Luther once said, "Jesus Christ takes our place. In a *wonderful exchange* he takes upon himself all men's debts and guilt before God. He is driven to this by his love; and in his love is God's love and mercy toward sinners." In other words, Christ's death on Calvary's cross was meant to remove guilt entirely, not produce it.

Isaiah's response to having his guilt removed was to say, "Here am I. Send me!" That, by the power of the Spirit, should be our response also—to understand, once again, that God has called us into this ministry with words of love and forgiveness so that we, in turn, can share that same love and forgiveness with our students. The motivational force that he uses to bring us into his service is far more powerful than guilt. It's called divine *love.* As you enter the classroom this week, think about the cross—the empty cross. Your sins and mine are gone, washed away in our Savior's own lifeblood. Make sure your students know that the burden of their sins was also done away with when Jesus carried them to his death.

It wasn't that long ago when everything—every business, every shop, every school—would close down for three hours on Good Friday. Just about everything came to a halt. It was a time set aside for personal and private reflection—a few hours to meditate on the meaning of that terrible and awesome day. You don't see that much anymore. Most people keep going from noon till 3:00 P.M. like it's just another day. It's not a regular day though. It's the day when our guilt was taken away. It's the day to know more fully how high and wide and deep the river of God's love runs.

These verses in Isaiah were part of an extraordinary vision that Isaiah experienced. In vivid detail he describes what God's holy throne room is like. There's smoke to signify his holiness. There are angels serving him. And the whole earth shakes and trembles at the Lord's awesome majesty. It's really a remarkable picture. But it's so profound that you begin to understand why any person who would find himself or herself in God's presence would have good reason to fear being consumed. What worm of a man would dare to believe he had a right to stand there in the almighty and holy presence of the righteous Lord God? The key is in recognizing that what Isaiah saw and heard was not the whole essence of God's great majesty. There was more. Much more! There, in the inner sanctum of God's own house, an undeserving Isaiah found relief from his guilty conscience from a loving and forgiving Savior-God. That's the wonder and the miracle of Holy Week!

Meditate on that this week! And then, in the spirit of Isaiah's willingness to answer God's call, become recommitted to saying, "Here am I. Send me!"

Easter

More Than Conquerors

> No, in all these things we are more than conquerors through him who loved us. For I am convinced that neither death nor life, neither angels nor demons, neither the present nor the future, nor any powers, neither height nor depth, nor anything else in all creation, will be able to separate us from the love of God that is in Christ Jesus our Lord. *Romans 8:37-39*

This past weekend was the end of the annual ritual called March Madness for the NCAA basketball championship. I was impressed by many of the winning and losing coaches and players who, during the tournament, were able to coach and perform with character and sportsmanship. Even though they were all good teams—many were conference champions—they embraced, rather than flaunted, their successes and chose to be more than winners. They chose to be ambassadors of the game and their schools.

I believe much the same can be said of Christian educators. They embrace their salvation. One might say that they are redeemed, restored, and ready.

Paul's words to the Romans have always intrigued me. What does it mean to be "more than conquerors"? If you are a conqueror, what else is left? The work of conquering has been done for us already. Jesus accomplished that through his death and resurrection. That was the hard part—the part we couldn't do. But to embrace our victorious roles as conquerors, you and I must use our newfound freedom in Christ's work to share God's love with others. We do this with confidence, sure that our efforts will be blessed.

Paul reassures us that nothing will separate us from the love of God. Do you know how big a word *nothing* really is? The list that the apostle provides is profoundly comprehensive. Read it again, and consider the difficulty we have in just comprehending each of the things Paul has included there. These are dynamic forces that are so cosmic that no human being can fully understand them. Yet none of them can penetrate the bond that holds us in our Savior's protective and loving arms.

"The strife is o'er the battle done; now is the victor's triumph won!" You and I share in that victory. We are already conquerors. Now, since Paul reminds us that we are never going to be separated from the author of that victory, we can also be "more than conquerors."

Easter

Ups and Downs

Therefore, since we have been justified through faith, we have peace with God through our Lord Jesus Christ, through whom we have gained access by faith into this grace in which we now stand. And we rejoice in the hope of the glory of God. Not only so, but we also rejoice in our sufferings, because we know that suffering produces perseverance; perseverance, character; and character, hope. And hope does not disappoint us, because God has poured out his love into our hearts by the Holy Spirit, whom he has given us. Romans 5:1-5

In one of my final years of coaching varsity girls' basketball, we were in a regional game where a victory would send us to the state tournament. By halftime we had built a 22-point lead. In the locker room we were outwardly cautioning ourselves against overconfidence. Inwardly we were patting ourselves on the back. Then the second half brought us back to reality . . . so much so that the game was tied at the end of regulation time. We were facing overtime, knowing we had blown a seemingly insurmountable lead. As time ran down in overtime, the game remained tied. Then, at the buzzer, one of our players hit a basket to win the game. Pandemonium ensued; we were headed to state! From the anticipation of greatness to the depths of despair to the surety of victory—all within two-and-a-half hours.

The disciples must have experienced some similar emotional highs and lows in that week we now call holy. From the absolute high of Palm Sunday to the overwhelming chasms of fear on Good Friday and then back to the remarkable victory of Easter. They were so sure they had it all figured out, then disaster struck, only to be closely followed by the exultation of the resurrection.

Have you ever had days like that? Weeks? Years? It's almost as if someone doesn't want us to have it too good. The apostle Paul felt that God had placed a "thorn in [his] flesh" (2 Corinthians 12:7) to keep him humble. Do you ever have the tendency to blame God for some particular thorn in your life?

Maybe your thorn is a student or a fellow faculty member that drags you down. Maybe it's a health issue or a financial concern. Personal family problems are familiar thorns that can crush even those of us who are most resilient. How easy it is to take these down times and let them influence our everyday lives. When we see sin all around us, when we recognize sin within us and feel the effects of that sin in our lives, it is easy to drift to low points that are impossible to get out of on our own.

Easter, on the other hand, lifts us up to soaring heights. Like that winning shot in overtime, Christ turns the impending defeat of the grave into the biggest win of all time.

Unfortunately, it sometimes takes a while for the reality of that to sink in. Sometimes the numbing drudgery of life can make us forget that because of Jesus' resurrection, each day is truly a new day in which we can once again fulfill our calling as children of God.

So jump up and down for joy this Easter. Experience the exhilaration of Christ's comeback over death. God never lets us lose. What a sweet victory!

Easter

Looking Ahead

Our fathers disciplined us for a little while as they thought best; but God disciplines us for our good, that we may share in his holiness. No discipline seems pleasant at the time, but painful. Later on, however, it produces a harvest of righteousness and peace for those who have been trained by it. Hebrews 12:10,11

When I was young, I thought of Holy Week as a time of innumerable church services. Okay, they weren't really innumerable; there were just a lot of them. From Palm Sunday to Maundy Thursday to Good Friday to Easter Vigil to Easter Sunday— they just kept happening! The only one I really looked forward to was Easter Sunday. Not only was it the most joyous of the services, it also meant that the marathon was over and that it was time for Easter baskets!

As I grow older, I realize that another reason I look forward to that service is because I'm simply looking ahead to the happy ending. I don't want to dwell on the rest of the story. Spending the time in worship, especially on Maundy Thursday and Good Friday, makes me confront myself on a level at which I'm not always comfortable. Those days make me acknowledge Christ's suffering and death. Those days make me look in the mirror. I never like what I see staring back at me.

If I could skip over those days, I might be able to ignore the fact that I am the reason for Jesus' suffering and death. Of course, we would do ourselves and others a tragic disservice if we were to gloss over the days leading up to Easter. It is the well-trained who find themselves mature in their relationship with God.

Part of that training is placing ourselves in Gethsemane with Christ, seeing him suffer, and standing at the foot of the cross, where we helped put him. Easter can be so much more fulfilling and meaningful when we choose to look inward first and forward later.

We can only appreciate the words of the Easter hymn, "This joyful Eastertide away with sin and sorrow," if we have felt the weight of our own sins and the sorrow that accompanies seeing our Savior suffer and die. Ask God's Spirit to lead you to a meaningful and uplifting Easter celebration that includes the introspection of all those days leading up to the glorious Easter victory.

Easter

Rejoice in the Lord

Rejoice in the LORD, *you who are righteous, and praise his holy name. Psalm 97:12*

    In the last six weeks or so, there have been a lot of athletes rejoicing. High school state championships in boys' and girls' basketball, wrestling, and swimming have taken place. The NCAA championships in the same sports have been happening with people watching from all around the world. The latest way to show pride is to lift your jersey and show your school's name to your fans and the opposing teams. In some postgame interviews, athletes and coaches thank God or their families for getting them to that place. I remember when a young Mohammed Ali became the first athlete to publicly thank his god (Allah) for giving him the victory.

    Not long ago we celebrated the victory of Easter. We dressed up and publicly demonstrated our joy in that day. Perhaps the luster of that day has faded a little since then. Perhaps we have become a bit less joyful as we have become preoccupied with the end of another school year. Going to church and keeping up with our personal prayers and devotional lives may seem a little more difficult when the promise of a joyful Easter Sunday is not on the horizon till next year.

    I recently returned from a national teachers' convention where, along with many other educators, I participated in worship, sectionals, and fellowship. I often feel quite humbled at these sorts of gatherings. I look at the many other educators who seem to be living lives of joy, who love to teach, whose very lives reflect effervescent joy. By my own standards, I fall short of that so many times. I am easily distracted by the challenges of life and quite often am not rejoicing in the Lord.

I must return to the Easter story. Because of Easter and, subsequently, because of my baptism into the family of God, I am righteous. According to the words of this psalm, the righteous are to rejoice in the Lord. Don't rejoice *because* of the Lord, or *with* the Lord, but *in* the Lord. He is in us, and we are in him thanks to the Spirit's working in our lives. That is the life that is ours because of Easter.

When we are in the Lord, we never need to feel inadequate in our lives. When we are in his Word and are making worship part of our lives, we are rejoicing in the Lord.

After seven or eight months of a school year, it is easy to get worn out. Let's face it, that much time with the same people would wear anyone out. It's easy to get on one another's nerves as we deal with another late assignment, another dress code violation, or another day with that coworker who knows just how to irritate us. We look forward to a break. But it's hard to rejoice when we look for earthly reasons to rejoice. When we acknowledge the role of Christ in our lives, when we once again accept our righteousness, thanks to God's Easter victory, then we can truly rejoice.

Over the next few weeks, turn your faith relationships up a notch. Remember the joy that is ours through Christ Jesus; literally re-joice. Commit yourself to worship, prayer, devotion, and Bible reading.

Find a small group or a person you can talk with about your faith. You have been made righteous, even on those days when you may not feel like it. That's reason enough to rejoice in the Lord.

Spring/Easter

Cheer Up!

Be joyful always; pray continually; give thanks in all circumstances, for this is God's will for you in Christ Jesus. Do not put out the Spirit's fire; do not treat prophecies with contempt. Test everything. Hold on to the good. Avoid every kind of evil. May God himself, the God of peace, sanctify you through and through. May your whole spirit, soul and body be kept blameless at the coming of our Lord Jesus Christ. The one who calls you is faithful and he will do it.
1 Thessalonians 5:16-24

It's that time of the school year again. You know what I mean? That time when if it's 70 degrees and sunny, I'd rather be outside doing anything else. And if it's 40 degrees and cloudy, I can't wait for school to be over and summer to be here. It's that time of the school year when everyone starts to get on my nerves—students, faculty, administration—everybody. Just let me be grumpy, because it's time for school to be done!

It's probably normal to get dragged down by the monotony of everyday life. I recently read an anecdote about Martin Luther. In his later years, it seems Luther was often overcome by bouts of depression. When he was down, everyone around him was prone to having bad days as well. This got so bad that his wife, Katy, decided to teach Martin a lesson. While he was out one day, Katy dressed herself in a drab, depressing way as if she were in mourning. When Luther returned, he asked Katy why she was outfitted for a funeral. Katy told her husband that she was sad because her Lord

Jesus was dead. In his typical fashion, Martin told her she was a foolish woman; didn't she know Christ was alive and could never die? To which Katy replied, "Is that so? I thought that surely he was dead because you are always so distressed and unhappy." Point made. Luther realized he had forgotten about the central belief that should have kept a smile on his face.

When you look around at your classroom and the students, are you easily frustrated because things don't happen the way you expect? Is your life, or your career, not developing the way you had hoped it might? Do you ever wonder if God is really hearing your prayers? Is it that time of the year when you're ready for school to end? Do you have days when your demeanor, like Luther's, communicates a lack of joy? It happens to all of us. But at this time of the year, when nature seems to be recharging and getting ready for spring and summer, why not do a little recharging of your own? Celebrate your relationship with your Savior-God in regular worship. Attend the Sacrament. Remember your baptism. And spend some time meditating on God's Word. Remember, Christ has risen! Make it a point to reflect your joy for his victory. Find a moment every day in your classroom to make sure that your students realize it as well. Christ has risen. Alleluia!

We Proclaim Christ

We proclaim him, admonishing and teaching everyone with all wisdom, so that we may present everyone perfect in Christ. To this end I labor, struggling with all his energy, which so powerfully works in me. *Colossians 1:28,29*

Yikes, what a week! I was admonished by one colleague, questioned by another, discussed weariness with a couple more. On top of all that, we're trying to figure out a family schedule that includes a graduation, a concert, moving two kids home from college, family birthdays, Mother's Day, prom chaperoning, and one son traveling to China. All in the next four weeks! And, oh yeah, Paul reminds me that in the turmoil of this month, I am to *proclaim Christ.*

With work and social commitments, family time, doctor's appointments, yard work, and whatever else fills your calendar, this is a most hectic time of year in an already hectic lifestyle. And, yes, Paul is also telling you to proclaim Christ.

So, are we? . . . that is, are we proclaiming Christ? Do our words, actions, relationships, and priorities proclaim Christ? I've always felt that when we're truly on top of our game, proclaiming Christ comes naturally. Our existence as individuals, as busy human beings, should be inseparable from our existence as children of God. This is a hard concept to teach young people and is even harder to live out in our own lives. Witnessing does not always have to be a specific event; it is often more of a lifestyle.

There are those times when our sinful nature wants us to take a hiatus from proclaiming Christ. Paul struggled with this tendency. In Romans, the apostle wrote, "I do not understand what I do. For what I want to do I do not do, but what I hate I do" (Romans 7:15). And in the text for today's devotion, he said he was "struggling with all his energy," referring to the energy that God provides in the message of the gospel.

I mentioned to someone recently that I could walk away from full-time ministry because "I feel like I've put in my time with God." Before you grab some stones to throw at me, think about your weariness at this time of the year or at this point in your life. I'm not asking you to share my feelings, but I think I understand Paul's comments about struggling. Am I weary? tired? struggling? You bet I am. But I also have Jesus' words of promise: "Come to me, all you who are weary and burdened, and I will give you rest" (Matthew 11:28). Once in a while I forget that. Apparently Paul did as well.

As I look at my colleagues and fellow redeemed, I am heartened to see so many who do daily proclaim Christ. These are people who are empowered by God's love and forgiveness. We all struggle at times, like Paul. We all need to hear and experience the same gospel proclamation over and over again, even as we proclaim it to others with our words and in our lives.

You may recall singing the following hymn very early in the school year when we were filled with enthusiasm for the teaching tasks that lay before us. But the words are just as appropriate now when we struggle with just making it through the day.

With the Lord begin your task;
Jesus will direct it.
For his aid and counsel ask;
Jesus will perfect it.
Ev'ry morn with Jesus rise,
And, when day is ended,
In his name then close your eyes;
Be to him commended.
    from "With the Lord Begin Your Task"

May

Serve as Jesus Served

The end of all things is near. Therefore be clear minded and self-controlled so that you can pray. Above all, love each other deeply, because love covers over a multitude of sins. Offer hospitality to one another without grumbling. Each one should use whatever gift he has received to serve others, faithfully administering God's grace in its various forms. If anyone speaks, he should do it as one speaking the very words of God. If anyone serves, he should do it with the strength God provides, so that in all things God may be praised though Jesus Christ. To him be the glory and the power for ever and ever. Amen. *1 Peter 4:7-11*

    Not to be overly dramatic, but sometimes the end of the school year can seem like "the end of all things is near." Given the attitudes of many students, parents, and educators in May, it can seem like that.

    Peter's world was a tumultuous one filled with persecution and uncertainty. So Peter attempts to give advice to his readers on how to handle stress, uncertainty, a cloudy future, and maybe even the last days of school.

    "Be clear minded and self-controlled." Tough to do on some of these days, isn't it? Keep your calling in mind. Why has God put you where you are, doing what you do? Focus on that calling, and keep your eyes on Jesus.

    "Love each other deeply, because love covers over a multitude of sins." In other words, keep on forgiving. Forgive that student who drives you nuts, that family member or coworker with that annoying habit, those parents who haven't been very helpful this year.

"Offer hospitality to one another without grumbling." Hospitality can mean different things. Maybe we just need to be a little nicer to people during some of these times when we really don't feel like it. Maybe we have to try to understand where students and parents are coming from during these hectic times. Maybe we really do need to offer help to students before or after school. Maybe there are coworkers who just need a little encouragement to get them through these last few weeks. The chances for hospitality are all around us.

"Use whatever gift he has received to serve others . . . with the strength God provides, so that in all things God may be praised." *Serving,* in it's basic form, means putting others first. That may seem hard at times. But God has blessed all of us with gifts that are designed to help others, not exalt ourselves. Serving as Jesus serves means not taking credit; it means looking for those who need to be served; it means being humble; it means relying on the strength of God; it means praising God through our actions. That's a tough order to fill. But when God called us through Baptism and poured out his Spirit on us, he did it knowing we could serve by modeling our service after Jesus' service, the perfect model. And the beauty is that God provides us with the strength to do that, even in the toughest of times.

Serving as Jesus served means putting our students first, whether they are 4 years old or 18 years old. It means putting them first, whether we're having a good day or a bad day. It means putting them first, even at those times when we'd rather be anywhere else.

The good news is that there are only a few weeks left in the school year. The bad news is that we only have a few weeks to show, by our actions and words, that we can be servants to the young people God gave us this year. The bad news is, we're tired; the good news is that God gives us the strength to be servants.

As the days and hours count down in this school year, let your goal as redeemed and forgiven Christian educators be to *serve as Jesus served.*

An Audience of One

One of the teachers of the law came and heard them debating. Noticing that Jesus had given them a good answer, he asked him, "Of all the commandments, which is the most important?" "The most important one," answered Jesus, "is this: 'Hear, O Israel, the Lord our God, the Lord is one. Love the Lord your God with all your heart and with all your soul and with all your mind and with all your strength.' The second is this: 'Love your neighbor as yourself.' There is no commandment greater than these." "Well said, teacher," the man replied. "You are right in saying that God is one and there is no other but him. To love him with all your heart, with all your understanding and with all your strength, and to love your neighbor as yourself is more important than all burnt offerings and sacrifices." When Jesus saw that he had answered wisely, he said to him, "You are not far from the kingdom of God." And from then on no one dared ask him any more questions.
Mark 12:28-34

A couple of years ago, the Fellowship of Christian Athletes used the theme "Audience of One" for their summer sports camps. The FCA tried to help players and coaches understand that athletics could be played not for the accolades but to the glory of God. This got me thinking about *for* whom we are in the business of education. Who's our audience? The obvious answer might be the *students.* But for some it may be the parents, the administration, a congregation, or a board of education. Do we teach for the accolades? Do we hope that by speaking or publishing or by pushing our school to greater heights that our constituents will finally give us the credit we deserve?

It is common practice in many team sports that when a key moment in the game approaches, the opposing fans try to create an atmosphere of chaos to cause doubt in the performer's mind. Coaches will often take time-outs to "ice" the athlete into failing. It takes an overwhelming amount of concentration and single-mindedness on the mission at hand for the athlete to be successful. If the athlete dwells on the wrong audience, he or she may fail.

It's not that different for us in education. If we forget that we too have an audience of One, we can be easily distracted by the periphery of our daily lives. The stresses of the end of the school year and the students who "drive us nuts" can be distractions of major proportions. If we each see that our life's work is to be done to the glory of the One, it makes each day a little easier. When we stop looking for the pat on the back or the thanks from a student or family to give us justification for what we are doing, then, and only then, will we find true satisfaction.

Playing for an audience of One is not without its challenges. When we fail, the failure will still be acutely felt. Our desire to show gratitude cannot be confused with the desire to earn God's love. Yet we also know that this audience is more loving than the most dedicated fan could ever be. His forgiveness is overwhelming, and his love never ends. What other audience is like that?

The next time you step into your workplace, go remembering your audience. It's the One who has called you to be his own. Through the power of his Spirit, you too can focus on an audience of One.

May

Upheld by His Hand

If the Lord delights in a man's way, he makes his steps firm; though he stumble, he will not fall, for the Lord upholds him with his hand. *Psalm 37:23,24*

    I don't remember exactly how old I was when I learned to ride a bike. It happened in the alley behind our house on the south side of Milwaukee. Our family had a timeworn tradition (one that I would later reprise with my sons): my dad would run behind me with one hand on the bike as I tried to master the art of the two-wheeler. When I looked back, I would notice he was no longer helping me and then promptly careen into a bunch of garbage cans. There was no apparent physical damage, but I did manage to split my pants. Eventually, I mastered that little 20-inch blue bicycle and learned to treasure the freedom it gave me.

    While the analogy is not perfect (I did, after all, fall), our Father in heaven "makes [our] steps firm" as we try to keep our balance in life. What I really appreciate now about that incident with the bike is that my dad let me stumble; he let me fall. I'm sure he could have kept going longer with his hand on the back of the bike, but he knew that eventually I'd have to do it on my own.

    This story about my father helps me remember the many times both of my parents let me stumble. Yet the falls were few because they were there to help. I suppose they could have kept me on some sort of leash that would have prevented me from stepping out and experiencing a nasty tumble or two. But then it's likely I would never have learned to ride the bike.

The author of this psalm, King David, saw God in the same way. He understood that God is not a controlling God who keeps us from stepping out on our own. David stumbled in his life too, badly. Yet he felt secure in knowing that God was there to help him continue on.

There are people who feel that God's plan for them involves running in place rather than taking some firm steps. There are parents who refuse to let their children grow up—they continue to plan their entire lives for them, even when they are no longer kids. They forget how important it is for immature people to overcome their fears in order to continue to grow and mature.

With the end of the school year approaching, you and I may feel like giving up. We're tired. The thought of going out there and stumbling or falling is not very appealing at all. We've fallen too many times already. There are times when all of us would rather stay on our tricycles, feeling confident with three wheels on the ground. Yet God is calling us to step out and take some firm steps, knowing that we may stumble but, more important, knowing that he is there watching over us throughout the process.

Most young graduates are facing very uncertain futures. They may be brimming with confidence, yet the challenges loom. They want to look back and see someone holding them up. In an earthly way, that may be you or me, their parents, or an aunt or uncle. But in a spiritual way, they need to see their Lord Jesus right there beside them, encouraging them, upholding them, guiding them. Remind them today that they have a heavenly Father, who has promised to be there with them as they take those important new steps into unfamiliar and uncertain futures.

May

They Just Don't Get It!

When they had finished eating, Jesus said to Simon Peter, "Simon son of John, do you truly love me more than these?" "Yes, Lord," he said, "you know that I love you." Jesus said, "Feed my lambs. "Again Jesus said, "Simon son of John, do you truly love me?" He answered, "Yes, Lord, you know that I love you." Jesus said, "Take care of my sheep." The third time he said to him, "Simon son of John, do you love me?" Peter was hurt because Jesus asked him the third time, "Do you love me?" He said, "Lord, you know all things; you know that I love you." Jesus said, "Feed my sheep. I tell you the truth, when you were younger you dressed yourself and went where you wanted; but when you are old you will stretch out your hands, and someone else will dress you and lead you where you do not want to go." Jesus said this to indicate the kind of death by which Peter would glorify God. Then he said to him, "Follow me!" Peter turned and saw that the disciple whom Jesus loved was following them. (This was the one who had leaned back against Jesus at the supper and had said, "Lord, who is going to betray you?") When Peter saw him, he asked, "Lord, what about him?" Jesus answered, "If I want him to remain alive until I return, what is that to you? You must follow me." Because of this, the rumor spread among the brothers that this disciple would not die. But Jesus did not say that he would not die; he only said, "If I want him to remain alive until I return, what is that to you?" *John 21:15-23*

It's really frustrating, isn't it? You spend a whole year trying to teach your students something, and they still don't get it. Or maybe it's your kids at home—when will they learn how to put the dishes

153

away correctly? Or maybe it's your spouse who still doesn't do things the way you want. And how about those parents who still don't get what a healthy snack is or how it's also their responsibility to help their kids in school? Then there's the person who, no matter how good things are for him or her, always wants more. Maybe you have some families like that in your ministry or maybe you work with a person like that. There always seems to be that one person who knows how to ruin a momentous time with a poor attitude. Well, add the disciples to your list.

Our reading gives us a glimpse of what should have been a great time. It was only days after Easter, and Jesus showed up for a barbeque on the beach—plenty of fish, lots of laughter, fun, and good times all around. To top it off, Jesus had forgiven Peter and had restored him to the status of disciple. But then Jesus told Peter something rather cryptic about being "dressed." Peter, who should have been thrilled about being back with Jesus, immediately wanted to know what would happen to John. Then the rest of the disciples got in on it by starting up rumors about John's not dying. Were those the same guys who just days before had been huddled together wondering what had happened to Christ? Were they so shortsighted that they were missing real joy by letting their petty jealousies overwhelm them . . . again?

I don't know about you, but there's a lot of these men in me. Easter's not even three weeks behind me, and I've already forgotten most of the joy that comes with it. My life has returned to a normal routine. With the end-of-the-school-year chaos at hand, it's also an easy time to forget that Christ has forgiven me and has called me just as he did with Peter. Instead, I let petty jealousies and worries cloud the joy of my call. Maybe I worry about how much money someone else makes or that someone else seems to be the principal's favorite. Maybe I think something in next year's plans is particularly unfair to me or that I'm being asked to work harder than my coworkers.

What it comes back to, again, is that I'm at odds with God's plans. Just as Jesus needed to put the disciples in their places, so I also need to hear that once in a while. The real joy in my life is that Christ is part of it. His resurrection means that I will rise to immortality. His death means that my sins were washed away. In spite of my own flaws, errors in judgment, and sinful weaknesses, Christ continues to forgive me. He also gently reminds me, through Scripture readings like this, that my concern should be for those I've been called to minister to and with.

As the school year draws to a close, it is a good time to be reminded of that again. Even when I want to shout out, "They just don't get it!" it's important for me to remember that I do *have it.* I have the love and forgiveness of a wonderful God. And that is more than enough for me.

May

Is Enough Ever Enough?

He said to them: "It is not for you to know the times or dates the Father has set by his own authority. But you will receive power when the Holy Spirit comes on you; and you will be my witnesses in Jerusalem, and in all Judea and Samaria, and to the ends of the earth." Acts 1:7,8

A couple weeks before my grandmother died, I drove her back to the Lutheran Home where she lived. During the trip she related to me how she wasn't afraid to die, but she said she wasn't sure she had done enough with the opportunities God had given her. She wasn't talking about doing enough to earn a place in heaven, she was talking about being the ambassador for Christ she felt she should have been. This was coming from a 90-year-old woman who had been a Lutheran elementary teacher until retirement, a Christian wife, mother, and great-grandmother who had seen seven children and grandchildren go into full-time church work. In her late 80s she had organized and led Bible classes for other residents at the home where she lived. This was in addition to all the years of service to her congregations. *Didn't do enough?* I get tired just thinking of all the things she did and the many people her faith influenced.

This week I thought of what my grandma said on that drive. I was looking at the list of our graduates this year and realized we had a student who would graduate after four years at our school who was never a member of a congregation. It would be easy to say that he had received his spiritual nurture through chapel and religion class. The reality is that we, correction, *I* didn't do enough. Somewhere along the way we didn't send the message that being part of a church is something we value and that he should value as well. We just took his tuition money and apparently felt confident that his just being here would give the Holy Spirit a chance to work. For all I know, several teachers or students may have talked to him over the years. But I didn't.

Now guilt is not a good motivator. Yet what I find disturbing is that we found plenty of time to make sure this student had his academics in order, wasn't a discipline problem, and participated in school activities. If I take my call seriously, I need to find a way to get past the mere rhetoric of the classroom and into the reality of life.

I'd like to think this devotion is more than the latest version of a tired, old theme that goes something like this: "As Christians we need to do a better job of spreading the good news to others." But the inescapable fact is that, in my life, I have a call to reach out with the gospel to students. That's one of the things that makes our schools unique and our teachers different from secular educators.

It's obvious that we can never do enough. Thank God he forgives our slowness in seeing the opportunities he so often presents to us. We also pray for greater insight, wisdom, and energy to act when there is an opportunity to do so right before our eyes. And we can't stop looking for ways to do more. While there is still daylight, we need to be engaged in the harvest. When nighttime comes, the work will cease. My grandma knew that!

End of the School Year

Running Out of Time

It is written: "I believed; therefore I have spoken." With that same spirit of faith we also believe and therefore speak, because we know that the one who raised the Lord Jesus from the dead will also raise us with Jesus and present us with you in his presence. All this is for your benefit, so that the grace that is reaching more and more people may cause thanksgiving to overflow to the glory of God. *2 Corinthians 4:13-15*

When I have the opportunity to speak to our juniors' parents, I tell them they have a little over a year to say to their children whatever they think their kids still need to hear. Once they graduate and go off to the next stage of their lives, the opportunity to teach them daily lessons will be gone. Not that they'll stop listening. (They may have already done that.) Not as though they will never speak with their parents again, but things will change. From that juncture in life on, young people learn more through their own life experiences than from parents' words.

The same is actually true for us as Christian educators. There is a kind of urgency to the end of a long year. For some of our students, these few remaining days in the school year may be the last times we have a chance to have an impact on their lives. It's certainly not time to keep quiet, as Paul says in the reading. More than ever, this is a time to say what we believe. Many of the students that graduate from our school will be going on to public institutions of learning. These are places that have excellent academics but may not afford their teachers the open opportunity to share their faith.

Whether we are faculty, staff, or parents, we may feel pressure right now to get everything done before the end of the school year. Every last unit must be covered. Every topic must be broached. We need, however, to be careful to maintain the same priorities of which we reminded one another throughout the school year. Jesus said it this way: "Only one thing is needed" (Luke 10:42). For us it is not only a priority established for the sake of our own spiritual welfare, it is also a priority for witnessing to what God has done for us during the little time we have left with the students who will not be back next year.

Even with only a few days left, Paul's words ring true. We benefit from having at least one more opportunity during these last few days to look for a moment with one student, or many, to share our experiences as the saved children of a loving and merciful God. It may be the perfect moment to speak about the "one thing needed," which is Jesus.

We are running out of time. God has called you and has put you in the situation you're in for a reason. Speak about God's love for you. Pray for the opportunity and the courage in these final days of the school year to say what you believe.

End of the School Year

Celebrate God's Grace

"But the father said to his servants, 'Quick! Bring the best robe and put it on him. Put a ring on his finger and sandals on his feet. Bring the fattened calf and kill it. Let's have a feast and celebrate. For this son of mine was dead and is alive again; he was lost and is found.' So they began to celebrate." *Luke 15:22-24*

Tomorrow Jean and I head off to attend the graduation of our older son, Andrew. He has accomplished much in his four years in college, and it will be a time of real celebration as he embarks on the next stage of his life. But the joy of this occasion will be tainted with just a bit of sadness. Our relationship will change once again as family dynamics always change. Things will never be quite the same. It's a reminder too that I'm getting older. On the other hand, we have much to celebrate in life, don't we? We have parties to celebrate our accomplishments, our beginnings and endings, and even getting older.

All this raises a question in my mind. Special church anniversaries or maybe a baptism party may cause us to *think* about God's grace, but how do we really *celebrate* the gift of God's grace to us?

The father in the story of the lost son had it right. He completely understood why he was celebrating: "This son of mine . . . was lost and is found." That's what has happened to you and me. We were lost through our sinful flesh, and God "found" us. He reached out with his love and called us to himself, to be safe in his arms again. That's worth celebrating!

Look around your classroom today. Look around your house today or tonight. Don't just take in the people who are around you but look at them as the father looked at the prodigal son. These people join with you as examples of God's grace in action. They too were lost and now are found. God's love has made them part of a larger family—the family of his children. This is worth celebrating!

At this time of the year, there is a real tendency to forget the day-to-day work of teaching and to concentrate on the end—the end of a long, sometimes difficult, school year. It's good to see an end in sight. In spiritual terms, we all know that means an eternity of glory with Jesus. At the same time, seeing the finish line should not become such a distraction that we forget to celebrate the little everyday victories of our everyday lives in God's kingdom of grace. We are *redeemed* and *loved* and *found* children of God. Celebrate in your own way—say a prayer of thanks to God, mention to your class that you're ready to party and celebrate what you have seen God do in your life and in theirs.

God's grace is alive in you; share your faith in Christ and his redeeming work. Make your whole life a celebration—a time of joy. Satan will, no doubt, try to rain on your party. He will seek to accuse you of being a sinner. Don't let him! Your life of sin and guilt has been dealt with. Jesus took that burden on himself. You are one of God's party animals; his love and forgiveness power your party. This is a time to celebrate as you thank God for his grace.

End of the School Year

Forward in Faith

In keeping with his promise we are looking forward to a new heaven and a new earth, the home of righteousness. So then, dear friends, since you are looking forward to this, make every effort to be found spotless, blameless and at peace with him. *2 Peter 3:13,14*

There is an old coach's axiom about practice that goes something like "You either get better or you get worse, you never stay the same." The point for the athlete is that if you don't work hard at every practice, you'll become stagnant and lose your edge for competing.

Our lives as Christians are very similar. There is a real temptation to just tread water and be comfortable. If we apply the coach's axiom to our faith-lives, the real danger is that we'll lose ground instead of growing stronger. Obviously I'm not talking about doing more things to secure our places in heaven. We've already been assured of our places through Christ. But what about working at our devotional lives, our prayer lives, our witnessing, and living Spirit-directed lives?

Paul tells us in Philippians 2:12 that we need to "continue to work out your salvation with fear and trembling." That's a real challenge for many of us, especially at this time of the year. The end is in sight, and there's really no reason to work at anything. Most people see summertime as vacation time. Unfortunately, that vacation may include a break from our worship lives and from time spent in God's Word.

This text from 2 Peter talks about looking forward as a way to deal with the present. Surely life eternal with God is something to look forward to. However, the second verse reminds us to "make every effort" as we look forward. To work at our faith and make every effort will include looking for and accepting new challenges in our faith-lives.

Most educators know what challenges they're facing. Are there people in your life that are a challenge to your faith? Have you shared the love of God with them? Are you sensing that this year was more negative than positive? Try to find a few more of the blessings that the year has brought to your life. Maybe this was the best year you've ever had and looking forward fills you with concern because it seems like it just couldn't be this good again next year. Whatever the case, don't forget about today. We know that Jesus is our Savior in the past and future, but where we are today is here and now—in the present. Ask God for the strength to search out the challenges of today and to meet them by working out your salvation.

Your relationship with God has the potential to become closer and more intimate or you can slip farther from his loving arms. Today, what will it be?

Look forward to the glory that awaits you and all believers in Jesus. Look back to the good old days of years gone by and the blessings they brought into your life. But do it in faith, with eyes wide open for a present in which you are making every effort to be spotless, blameless, and at peace with God.

Graduation

A Different Kind of Commencement

> After his suffering, [Jesus] showed himself to these men and gave many convincing proofs that he was alive. . . . On one occasion, . . . when they met together, they asked him, "Lord, are you at this time going to restore the kingdom to Israel?" He said to them: "It is not for you to know the times or dates the Father has set by his own authority. But you will receive power when the Holy Spirit comes on you; and you will be my witnesses in Jerusalem, and in all Judea and Samaria, and to the ends of the earth." After he said this, he was taken up before their very eyes, and a cloud hid him from their sight. They were looking intently up into the sky as he was going, when suddenly two men dressed in white stood beside them. "Men of Galilee," they said, "why do you stand here looking into the sky? This same Jesus, who has been taken from you into heaven, will come back in the same way you have seen him go into heaven." *Acts 1:3-11*

The story of the Christ's ascension has become one of my favorite Bible stories. When I was young, the idea of Jesus flying up into the air coincided nicely with the beginning of space exploration. In my young mind, I supposed that Jesus just kept going higher and higher until he was out of the universe.

Today the picture I have of the ascension is very different. After 40 days of intermittent contact, the disciples had more time to prepare for Jesus' leaving them. Despite the fact that they kept gazing into heaven after Jesus left, I think they really understood what had happened.

As an educator, I especially appreciate the celebration of the ascension happening so close to the end of the school year. Our graduates are leaving for good; other students and the faculty are leaving for summer break. It seems like we need some guidance and words at such a time. The ascension experience can fit into our lives, and our students' lives, just as well as it fit into the lives of the disciples.

Jesus promised the disciples that his Spirit would come and give them a power that is truly divine. He kept that promise for his disciples . . . and for us. Through our baptisms, God called us to be his own, but he also empowered us to live as though we belonged to him.

When Jesus ascended, he gave his followers an explicit command—to make disciples of everyone they came into contact with, starting at home. This isn't a suggestion; it's a *comission*; it's marching orders to a waiting army of eager followers. We share in the adventure and the excitement of serving in Jesus' unit. It's a pitched battle all the way. With his power and resources of mercy and love, the promise of the ultimate victory is a secure one. We go forward, confident and assured of his word never to leave us or forsake us in our daily battles.

On that first Ascension Day, as the disciples continued to stare into the sky, searching for their Jesus, they were snapped back to reality by the words of an angel: "What are you waiting for? Jesus is gone ahead to prepare your heavenly reward. Now get to work!" We can't sit around and wait for things to happen. Time is precious. There are still people who don't know about their Savior. Unless we tell them, they will perish. What an awesome privilege God has given to each one of us to carry his saving truth wherever we go.

As our graduates leave, they will hear many words of encouragement, of wisdom, of advice. None are more meaningful than the commencement address that Jesus gave on that mountaintop. It was a commencement address of a different kind.

The word *commencement* means "beginning." It is really a celebration of a new beginning. For Christians, Jesus' ascension into heaven marks the beginning of a whole new era. And thank God that he's included you and me in his plans for all the excitement of going into a dying world with the only message that offers life. He knows the way. He shows the way. He is the way . . . the *only* way.

As we look forward to summer, as our graduates look forward to life after high school, we pray that we will all continue to be empowered and directed by God's Holy Spirit. With his power we can commence to meet every new challenge before us as his ambassadors for sharing the good news.

For Such a Time as This

"If you remain silent at this time, relief and deliverance for the Jews will arise from another place, but you and your father's family will perish. And who knows but that you have come to royal position for such a time as this?" Esther 4:14

Although the name of God is never mentioned in the book, Esther's is an extraordinary story of faith and the desire to follow God's will. At great risk to herself and her family, Esther sought to do what was right. At a critical moment in her life, when God's plan of bringing salvation to the world through the Jewish race seemed to have been in serious jeopardy, Esther recognized that she was there, at "such a time as this," for a divine reason. And with great courage and conviction, she made a dangerous decision that would eventually prove to be a defining moment in saving her nation (and God's plan) from ruin.

As I write, our school is within a couple of days of graduation. Many faculty members seem worn out, spent, ready for the end. There is also frustration with roadblocks to ministry, missed opportunities, needs being ignored. The air is electric with emotion—some of it positive, some quite negative—anxiety, joy, fear, frustration, exaltation, confusion, just to name a few. The desire to see the school year end may, in fact, be keeping us from embracing these last few days as opportunities for final chances to influence the young people God has placed into our care and nurture.

Esther's primary emotion was fear. There was a good chance that she could have been executed for stepping into the king's presence without an invitation. Esther had to overcome her fear in order to seize the moment God had put before her. The early disciples were so paralyzed by fear in the days that followed Easter that they locked their doors. The evil servant in Christ's parable was so afraid that he buried his talents rather than seeking opportunities to use them. In moments of great opportunity, you and I need to be careful about slamming doors shut and burying opportunities. We are here for such a time as these last few days of the school year.

Our personal struggles with physical, spiritual, or relational issues can create the kind of instability and chaos in our lives that Satan enjoys seeing. In such times we are especially vulnerable to the more negative emotions. Sometimes, in fear, we may overlook or even consciously ignore God's will. These moments could still happen today or tomorrow.

In fact, in the final analysis, with God every moment is "such a time as this." Every moment is another opportunity to meditate on his love for us or to say a prayer for his eternal presence and power or to seek reassurance in his enduring promises. Every moment is also a time to spend with those we love, with those whom God has placed in our lives at work or school or in our neighborhoods. They are all opportunities to express God's love through our words and actions.

Esther found joy when she put her faith into action. You and I can do the same. Blessed by God and his grace every day, you and I, and our students, can come to see all of our time as time for serving God by seeking to do his will.

May

Where's My Reward?

After this, the word of the LORD came to Abram in a vision: "Do not be afraid, Abram. I am your shield, your very great reward." *Genesis 15:1*

It's the time of the year when a lot of graduations and confirmations are taking place. Students of every age seem to be getting diplomas, from prekindergarten graduates to students getting graduate degrees. In a way, all of them are receiving a reward. Even if that reward means they go on to something more challenging, like a job.

But what of those who helped them get to this point? I realize that the company line is that our reward is seeing our students graduate, but that doesn't always seem like much of a reward for all of the effort it has taken to get them this far.

From a different standpoint, I sometimes wonder what the reward is for years of dedication to church work. Perhaps I'm the only called worker who lets these seeds of doubt and dissatisfaction creep into my everyday life. Sometimes I feel like I've done everything I was supposed to do; and yet the rewards seem like slim pickin's. I am a living example of the rich young man in Matthew chapter 19 who professed to keeping all of the commandments yet went away from Christ unsatisfied because he wasn't up to the final challenge. While I would never claim to have kept all the commandments, there is part of me that wants to say, "Hey, what about me? I've dedicated myself to church work—what else do I have to do to get a break around here?" God, forgive my impertinence at such times. Again, I know the answer is that our rewards will come in heaven, but too many times I don't have the patience to wait for that.

My grandmother, who spent her whole working life as a Lutheran teacher, may have had doubts, but I never heard her articulate them. Till her dying day she was still working to spread the good news of Christ. I think her secret was that she didn't have to wait for her reward in heaven; she knew she already had it.

Her reward, and ours, is that *God* is the reward. Just as the Lord said to Abram, so he says to us, "I am . . . your very great reward." The love, the forgiveness, the comfort, and the joys that are ours because of our Savior's work on our behalf are our rewards. My reward is that I can handle the challenges of life because I have been given the confidence that God is with me all the way. My reward is that I can handle those moments when I doubt because God strengthens me. My reward is that because of my baptism, the Spirit will help me out of the deep valleys that life takes me through. My reward is that his peace will guide me through that moment when my eyesight dims and death itself threatens to overtake me. My reward is the Word made flesh and dwelling in me by the power of his Spirit. My reward is my Savior, and he is here now! I don't have to wait for a reward in heaven; I've already got it. And I didn't do anything to earn it. What a deal! In fact, there's no way that I ever could have earned it. My reward is that Christ Jesus came to do everything that God required of me—everything that would have been impossible for a sinner like me to accomplish.

There are those teachers who will say their rewards come from the smiles on their students' faces or the satisfaction in knowing they have helped students reach the "next level." There are also those who will say their reward is in bringing another child or family to Christ. They're right! Those are rewarding moments. But the next time I feel as though life hasn't been fair to me, I hope to remember that my true reward is with me all the time.

General

Say What?

Now there were staying in Jerusalem God-fearing Jews from every nation under heaven. When they heard this sound, a crowd came together in bewilderment, because each one heard them speaking in his own language. Utterly amazed, they asked: "Are not all these men who are speaking Galileans? Then how is it that each of us hears them in his own native language? Parthians, Medes and Elamites; residents of Mesopotamia, Judea and Cappadocia, Pontus and Asia, Phrygia and Pamphylia, Egypt and the parts of Libya near Cyrene; visitors from Rome (both Jews and converts to Judaism); Cretans and Arabs—we hear them declaring the wonders of God in our own tongues!" Amazed and perplexed, they asked one another, "What does this mean?" *Acts 2:5-12*

 Did you ever say something to a student or a parent and then find out later that he or she thoroughly misunderstood what you said? I recently ran across this paragraph in an article I was reading: "When Coca-Cola went into China, they were determined to use a symbol that phonetically represented the sounds of their name. It was only after their marketing campaign was a failure that Coke learned that their new symbol translated, 'Bite the wax tadpole.' When they changed their name to mean, 'May the mouth rejoice,' they began to sell their product. When Chevrolet took the Nova to Latin America, they neglected the fact that in Spanish the name meant 'Won't go.' Pepsi's campaign in Taiwan translated the invitation to 'Come alive with Pepsi' into 'Pepsi brings your ancestors back alive from the grave.' Eastern Airline's slogan 'We earn our wings daily' promised in Spanish that passengers would arrive at their destination as angels. Parker Pen made even more extravagant claims in Flemish, asserting that their newly created leak proof cartridges would prevent unwanted pregnancies. But perhaps most stunningly, Frank Perdue's slogan, 'It takes a tough man to make a tender chicken,' announced in Spanish that 'It takes a virile man to make a chicken affectionate.'"

While these are humorous anecdotes, they really point out how easy it is to be misunderstood, even when we're sure we're saying the correct things. What a blessing it was for the disciples to know that through the power of the Spirit they were understood correctly on that Pentecost Day. To know that by the grace of God the message of salvation would be so clearly heard that thousands would be baptized had to create a sense of wonder and accomplishment that we could only hope to imagine. Or can we do more than imagine this?

As called teachers of the Word, we too through the power of the Spirit and the grace of God have the opportunity to clearly articulate the story of Christ's love in our lives. Each day we have the opportunity to teach children about salvation that is theirs in Jesus and his cross. It's easy to look at what happened on Pentecost and feel like we're just not doing the job—when's the last time you saw thousands baptized at once? Yet we have little victories all the time.

You and I won't necessarily see the times when the Spirit comes alive in our students. God isn't obliged to provide us with detailed reports of his Spirit's work in the hearts of our students. We will go on complaining about the music they listen to, the clothes they wear, and their lack of respect. We may even complain that they don't hear what we have to say. But quietly God is at work in them.

One has to wonder if the disciples may have felt the same way as they looked over the mixed group of people assembled in Jerusalem on that first Pentecost. It was a veritable plethora of races, dialects, and ethnicities that confronted them. People that didn't always dress as they did, may not have seemed to be listening, and, up to this point, perhaps saw no reason to respect the disciples. Yet by God's grace and the power of his Spirit, the people heard a message that was so profound it changed their lives.

The Spirit told Jesus' disciples to speak; he then opened the ears and hearts of the people to hear and understand. He has called you and me to do the same thing: to be bold, to speak out. Pray that he also opens the ears and hearts of those around us to hear and understand the truth, that they may have life.

Embrace Them; Then Let Them Go

"My children, I will be with you only a little longer. You will look for me, and just as I told the Jews, so I tell you now: Where I am going, you cannot come." Simon Peter asked him, "Lord, where are you going?" Jesus replied, "Where I am going, you cannot follow now, but you will follow later." John 13:33,36

A couple of weeks ago, I watched from the stage as another group of graduates strode confidently down the aisle at the beginning of another graduation. It was a scene played out all across the country many times during the last few weeks. From kindergarten to graduate school, students had reached the end of their formal education for the year, some for life. Some of them were more ready than others. And some were more confident than others. But they were all moving on.

It is always a time of mixed emotions. Parents are proud, yet often sad as they watch their children grow into the next facet of life. Teachers may feel some relief, some pride, and perhaps also a twinge of sadness. Hearing "Pomp and Circumstance" can touch tender emotions in even the toughest of us as we remember graduations in our past. In the inevitable congratulations that follow, there are many hugs, much gathering and partying. But that also must end, and we move on.

As Christian teachers and parents, we need to embrace an idea that is somewhat foreign to everything that has happened up to this point. It's the idea of letting them go, permiting our young people the freedom to move on into mature lives without authority figures looking directly over their shoulders. We need to let our students and children know of God's great love and rich grace for them. We need to let them feel the comfort and security that comes from being in God's embrace. We need to communicate to them the power they have in God's Holy Spirit. We need to demonstrate to them the importance of sharing the Word of God with others. We need to convince them of the urgency of letting God rule in their lives now. We need to help them see that their spiritual lives are not separate entities from their everyday lives. And then we need to let them go.

Christ spoke these words of the text, that his Word would remain and that one day he would come again in power and victory. So he let the disciples know that it was time for them to go out into the world without his physical presence. They could not go, he would not go without giving them one more reassuring word that would let them know that he would be back soon to take them to be with him forever.

We'll miss our students. We may never see some of them again on this side of heaven. Our time together here on earth has ended. But we know that God will bless our efforts at sharing Jesus with them. They've had positive models for the Christian life in the days, months, and years we've been together. They have a picture of Jesus imprinted in their hearts that has a faint resemblance to you and me. We've had our time together to embrace them. And now we must let them go.

Send them off in God's protecting hand. Trust that the good work begun in them in Baptism and strengthened by the Holy Spirit working through educators like us will continue with them. Then stand back and admire God working in them as they grow in him and for him.